RUSSELL GRANT'S
1992 HOROSCOPES

Books by Russell Grant

Your Love Signs
Your Sun Signs
1992 Horoscopes

RUSSELL GRANT'S

1992 HOROSCOPES

TAURUS

21 April-21 May

VIRGIN

First published in Great Britain in 1991 by
Virgin Books
338 Ladbroke Grove
London W10 5AH

ISBN 0 86369 482 9

Illustrations by Maggie Keen

Typeset by Phoenix Photosetting, Chatham, Kent.
Printed in Great Britain by
Cox & Wyman Ltd, Reading, Berks.

CONTENTS

INTRODUCTION

Welcome to the latest edition of my astrological almanac, full of information about the starry trends coming your way in nectarine 1992!

If you've been wondering what the New Year has in store for you, then you need look no further than the packed pages of this book, for it contains all you need to know for an enjoyable, enterprising and successful annum. If you're a regular reader of my columns and books, then you'll know by now that astrology is all about forecasting the possible pitfalls, problems and possibilities indicated by the planets' positions and relationships in the heavens. It can't determine your destiny, because only you can do that by exercising your free will, but what it can do is point out all the good and bad vibes that are surrounding you. Then you can cash in on every opportunity that comes your way, or turn nasty or negative situations to your advantage by being prepared for them in advance. And there's a special section outlining your amorous, pecuniary and professional prospects over the coming year. Let's face it, we can all be wise after the event, but wouldn't it be better to be wise beforehand?

Speaking of sagacious subjects, have you ever worried that you're not tapping your true potential or making the most of your innate talents and aptitudes? If so, then turn to the first half of this book and soak yourself in the section telling you how to do just that, with the help of that generous giant Jupiter. What's more, if you've got a loved one who wants to cash in on all their capabilities and you know their birth date, then you're all set to help them find their true selves as well!

Communications are of prime importance in all our lives, but every now and then they seem to go up the spout, leaving us high and dry and wondering what went wrong. That's all thanks to the antics of mini Mercury, messenger of the gods and ruler of all our daily dealings. Well, with the help of my section on his movements throughout 1992, you'll be able to plot his planetary positions and discover how they'll affect you as he moves around the celestial set-up. Remember, forewarned is forearmed!

Wondering why a relationship's reached rock bottom, or want to know how you'll fare with someone you've just met? Then look no further than my chapters on the twelve Sun signs, and also my relationship guide, to learn everything you need to know about getting on with others. Want to know your lucky number, day of the week or birthstone? Then turn to my chart giving the traditions of astrology, and start reading!

If you're always wondering where to go on holiday, then why not let the stars give you a few hints? Turn to my travel guide to see which towns, cities and countries are ideal for your Sun sign. You could be in for a big surprise!

Once you've read all that, plus my day-by-day forecasts, you'll be all set for a propitious, providential and positive new year. Enjoy yourself!

RUSSELL'S GUIDE TO THE SUN SIGNS

ARIES – 21 MARCH–20 APRIL

Me, me, me, me! No, it's not an opera singer practising the scales, but the Arien catch-phrase. This is the first sign of the zodiac, and Ariens like everyone to remember that. (First come, first served, is the Martian motto.) And because this is such a fun-loving, frisky sign, Ariens can get away with it.

The positive side of Aries is like a scene from *The African Queen*, in which our intrepid explorers boldly go where only crocodiles have gone before. Ariens are active, alive, awake (usually), assertive and adventurous, hacking their way through the undergrowth of life like Marlon Brando in a steamy movie. (Yes, he's an Arien!) But they can take this exuberance to extremes. (They can take a lot of things to extremes!) Ariens can step out, putting their best feet forward (all four of them – well, they are animals!) and sinking up to their best end of necks in trouble.

Luscious Libra is the polar sign of assertive Aries, and these signs have a lot to learn from each other. Librans always put others first, which is something Ariens find almost impossible to do. In fact, a relationship between these two is their idea of heaven, because they both think about the Arien. (And of course, after 'Me', the Ram's favourite word is 'Ewe'!)

Sometimes, this can cause a contretemps in the course of true

3

love. Male Ariens may forget about the wife and six kids at home and gad about like a bachelor gay with a collection of conquests. Arien women may throw their weight about too, demanding new dresses and wanting to be taken to the best restaurants, even when their men haven't got two halfpennies to rub together.

Aries is ruled by Mars, the planet that gives them that gorgeous get-up-and-go, that delicious drive and determination. (As long as they're not determinedly driving all over delicious *you*!) Mighty Mars rules Scorpio, too, when he shares the limelight with powerful Pluto. Then he can make Scorpios furtive and underhand, but when he's in open Aries, it's a very different story. Ariens can be so candid and frank that it's an excruciating experience to hear them. You can meet your Martian mate for a meal, and swan in, looking sensational. (Or so you think, you poor dear.) The Arien will take one look at you and say 'That frock makes you look fatter than ever.' (How can you then say that you've just lost two stone – and a pal in the process!)

There's something rather ingenuous about Aries. Because this is the first sign of the zodiac, Rams represent the babies of the celestial sky. Sometimes they're so naive and innocent it's astounding, and they'll dash off and do or say something really reckless. (Or just plain potty!) They can also have terrible temper tantrums, like a tirading toddler, and shout and scream till they're blue in the face. Assertive Ariens are so determined to get what they want that they'll let nothing stand in their way. They'll go on until it kills them.

Every sign has its own song, and the Arien's aria must be 'Let's Get Physical'. (Take that in any way you like. After all, they will!) Rams are imbued with enough physical energy to fill a whole football team (and a stand of supporters!). But, like children, they have to find positive pursuits in which to burn it all off. Ariens are full of fire, fun, vivacity, verve and virility. (Quite a captivating concoction, which can really go to your head!) But they can fritter away their fantastic physical fitness, and instead of having an active social, sports or sex life, turn to violence and vandalism. (Even the meekest and mildest mutton will show a strong side sometimes, and may bop you on the bonce for no apparent reason.) Some of these Martians can be all brawn and no brain, thinking with their fists – or any other part of the anatomy that springs to mind! (Ariens have powerful passions and strong sex drives!)

Ariens are like medieval knights, arrayed in armour and jousting for superiority. Their Fiery natures make them compulsively competitive, and determined to do battle. They have *got* to come first. Rams, lambs and sheep hate losing, whether at Ludo, life or love. (They'll just throw the dice for a six and start again.) When they see success slipping away, they'll fight tooth and claw, frightening off folk in their flocks. Watch out, watch out, there's a Ram about!

TAURUS – 21 APRIL–21 MAY

Taureans are very easy creatures to understand. They have very basic needs: male Bulls love grub and girls, and females of this sign adore food and fellas. Simple, isn't it?

Being the first of the Earth signs, Taurus symbolises rich, rolling fields of very dark brown earth waiting to be cultivated. The Sun sits in the sign of Taurus at Maytime, and so Taurus is linked with the ritual of May Day, the maypole, young maidens, and earthy, pagan customs and folklore.

Taureans are governed by their love of sensuality in all its forms, and some of them can go a mite mad and overindulge themselves, whether it's with sex or a simmering stew with delicious dumplings.

A lot of Taureans have very expressive, often deep-set eyes, that can put across their message better than a million Gemini words. I know one normally sensible, sane Capricorn girl who was reduced to a gibbering wreck when one of these Bulls looked at her across a crowded room. He didn't have to say a word – his eyes did all the talking. (I'd wondered why she suddenly blushed like a beetroot.)

Bulls hate change. They need to know that tomorrow will be the same as today, and that the day after tomorrow will be the same as a week next Wednesday. This is not a sign that is moved by challenge, but Bulls can show tremendous endeavour, patience, persistence and resoluteness.

I have many Taurean chums, and what I absolutely adore about them is that when you go to visit them, you will have barely opened the garden gate before they've offered you a cuppa and asked you if you've eaten. (Say no.) They can be wonderfully warm and welcoming, really making you feel at home, and wondering what they can give you that is theirs. (More stew?)

Ownership is very important to Taureans. Seeing a room full of furniture they've paid for, or a freezer full of food, makes them feel secure. However, negative Taureans can be so possessive and narrow-minded that they can class wives, husbands, kids and pets in the same category as the couch and the cooker and feel that they own them lock, stock and barrel.

To give you an idea of the good and bad sides of the Bull, a country said to be ruled by Taurus is the Emerald Isle. Think of the simple, relaxed way of life there, those glorious greens and beautiful browns of the Irish countryside; then think of the widespread bigotry over religion with both sides refusing to compromise, and you have Taurus at its worst.

In fact, one description of Taurus that you will hear time and time again is 'stubborn as a mule'. Certainly, Taurus is a Fixed sign, and Taureans can be as hard to shift as a sack of soggy cement, but I do think this so-called stubbornness is a wee bit overemphasised. Of course, there is a diabolical dose of dogged determination in the Taurean character, but these Bulls are not always as obstinate and obtuse as they are portrayed. In fact, if used positively, this steadfast streak can lead to persistence and determination. On the negative side, it can lead to rumbustious rows because of the Taurean's intransigence and inability to see another person's point of view.

But make no mistake. If used in the right way, fixity can be a wonderful thing. If Bulls want something slightly out of reach, they will put their heads down and charge (slowly) straight for it, eventually achieving their goal, even if it kills them in the process!

As you might expect from a sign that symbolises the countryside, often Taureans aren't very happy in the city – unlike Air or Fire signs, who like hustle and bustle. Taureans, on the other hand, need to live in a place where they can commune with nature, feeling the ground beneath their feet and seeing the sky above their heads. Bulls will be at their best in a verdant village, or a comfy crofter's cottage. City Bulls will have stacks of window boxes crammed with leafy flora, to give them that 'at home' feeling. Bulls' abodes will be warm and welcoming, unless they are going through a desperate disruption or change in their relationships.

Taureans rarely do anything quickly, choosing to take their time. If they're negative, they may prefer to pretend that their position, passionwise, is pootchy, when even the fly on the wall can see that it isn't. Eventually the world will crumble around their ears, when their amour ambles off with another. Everyone except the Bull will have seen exactly what was happening, and not be outraged at the outcome.

Taureans find it especially difficult to accept change in their emotional relationships, because fidelity and loyalty are paramount to them. But whether a Taurean likes it or not (probably not), changes of some sort or another will be inevitable in their lives, and the sooner they get used to the idea the better. The more they can make themselves cope with change, the less heartache they will have in the long run. I know many Taureans who have resisted an upheaval that was inevitable, and gone through hell and high water as a result.

Venus rules Taurus and Libra, endowing both signs with a love of beauty and a need for harmony, although they seek these ideals in different ways. When ruling Libra, Venus is lighter and more sanguine, but she's much deeper and richer in Taurus. Librans love Rodgers and Hammerstein, while Taureans will opt for opera. They love the beauty of flowers, the earth and all the good things in life, and with their classical, traditional outlook, can teach a lot of the more restless signs quite a lesson or two. So don't fall into the trap of thinking Taureans are simply bull-headed. They can be obstinate, though they would call it being strong-minded!

GEMINI – 22 MAY–21 JUNE

If you want to know how a Gemini ticks, sidle up to the one you're trying to puzzle out, start up a chatette, and then listen very carefully. Above the twinkling tones of the Twin twittering on, you may hear a weird whirring, combined with a couple of clicks. Yes? Well, congratulations, my dears, you have just heard the Gemini brain cells in action. And they are what make every Gemini tick.

The more astute Twins will actually admit to being aware of their Mercurial minds working. They can *feel* themselves thinking. Just imagine all those neurons neoning away inside their noddles. Geminis think so quickly that they leave some of the other signs standing. Everything they see and hear will pass through that brilliant brainbox and be stored away for future reference in the Geminian filing system.

If you're meeting a Gemini for the first time, you'll notice how nervously and quickly he or she moves. Even if the Twin is sitting talking to you, his or her eyes will be taking in everything in the

7

room, and everything about you. Even the egg stain on your tie and the fascinating fact that you're wearing odd socks!

Geminis have a very low boredom threshold, and you'll soon know if you've made them cross it. Their peepers will be poring all over the place and rarely popping back to you. (Apart from your egg stain, of course, because they'll be dying to ask you if it was boiled or fried.) Their fingers will begin to tap out tunes on the table, their feet will jiggle up and down, and they will become fantastically fidgety. This is a danger sign, and unless you can suddenly turn the conversation on to a different, more scintillating subject, to ignite their interest again, you may as well give up and go home. Otherwise you'll be written off as being too boring to bother with.

All Geminis have an elfin appearance, and look like potential pixies. It's rare for them to look like hobgoblins, because this is a very attractive sign, both mentally and physically. The typical Twin – male or female – is incredibly pretty in a boyish way, with alert, shining eyes and fine features.

Most Twins have a very fast way of talking, and may even start to stammer when excited. That may sound strange when you consider that Geminis are so glib and garrulous, and graced with the gift of the gab, but actually sometimes their minds move faster than their mouths, and you get a right old scramble coming out! Geminis love puns because it means they can play about with their favourite toys – words.

Every sign has its good and bad side, and Gemini is no exception. Positively, Geminis are incredibly lively, witty people, extremely articulate and natural communicators. But the reverse of that is the Twin who uses communications in the wrong way, and tells terrible lies (like Matilda's, they make one gasp and stretch one's eyes). Some Geminis like to bend the truth into real reef knots: they can be real Uri Gellers with words.

A lot of Geminis say to me, 'Oh, I'm two-faced, because I'm a Twin,' but I think they've got it wrong. The popular myth is that all Geminis are raving schizophrenics, or Jekyll and Hyde characters, being sweet as sugar one minute and ravening beasties the next. You have to look at Gemini's ruling planet, Mercury, to work this out. As it spins about the solar system, one side of it is always in darkness, and the other is always light. And it's the same with the Twins. When we talk of dark and light in a personality, we can mean a true schizophrenic, with two personalities in one mind, or simply someone, like a Gemini, who experiences a tremendous variety of emotions within *one* personality. Geminis can certainly have extremes of character, and on one level be alert, bright, chatty and chirpy, and on another, be so depressed they can't even find the words to describe how miserable they are.

Very often, Geminis can be desperately disappointed with the world. It can be such a dull place, full of such dreary people that Twins have to invent their own, brighter world to cheer themselves up. Geminian memories of events are always a slightly different version of what really happened!

If you understand this it'll help you to appreciate the Twins you know better. You should even feel a bit sorry for them, if you think about it. People who live in their heads that much are bound to be lonely, at least some of the time.

CANCER – 22 JUNE–23 JULY

Cuddle and caress a Cancerian you know, today! Crabs need to feel safe and secure, and to know that they are adored and amoured.

This is the sign of Moons and Junes – literally! Leo is led by the Sun, but Cancer is ruled by the other leading light of the zodiac, the Moon. Throughout history and legend, the Moon has always represented motherhood, and she rules the tides, menstruation, and everything else associated with the 28-day cycle. (No, it's not a new form of transport!) The Moon is the peaceful, passive, defensive drive within us, and in the natal chart she shows our maternal instincts, habits and childhoods, and whether we love or loathe our mums.

Generally speaking, Cancerians are ultra-protective, and that can mean they protect themselves as well as others. (Well, aren't crabs encased in shells?) A very good friend of mine says that if you think of a rocker, clad in chain mail and leather, looking fearfully ferocious, then try to imagine taking all that chain mail off, you'll find a very ordinary person underneath. And you can say exactly the same thing about Cancer the Crab. There they are, with that solid shell, that concrete coating, waving their pincers about provocatively, and pretending to be pugnacious. But get out the crab cracker and you have the main ingredient for a rather nice crab sandwich – sweet and soft! (Slap two slices of brown bread around them, quick!)

When you first meet a Cancerian, you will sense a hardness, tetchiness, and moodiness, as Crabs are always on the defensive! These are the folk who rush into the room and slap you round the face, just in case you're going to be nasty!

On a positive level, this is a devoted sign. Crabs have a fierce family feeling, can get quite clannish, and put their kith and kin at the centre of their universes.

Many Cancerian men tie the nuptial knot, but can't untangle the apron strings that bind them to their mums and dads. This can cause fantastic flare-ups within their marriages, because their wives feel upstaged by their mothers-in-law. And lots of Cancerian women spend almost all their weekends with their parents in the bosom (what a nice Cancerian word!) of their families, even when they've got a husband and six kids at home. (Maybe that's why!)

Crabs can remember what they had for breakfast on their second birthdays, but they can also remember when you last let them down. They will hurl back past slights, which happened many moons before, in the middle of a row. They also like to live in the past (ever seen a Crab in a crinoline?), and they're very traditional, and tremendous collectors of bits and bobs, especially if they are full of memories. (They call them mementoes. Other people call them tat.) And they hoard letters like mad! (A true Crab will have kept all the letters he or she has ever received from the age of six months onwards.)

You see, they hate to throw things away. (Just in case they come in handy.) A Cancerian friend of mine once went whizzing off to a jumble sale at eleven in the morning loaded with the memorabilia (another good Cancerian word) she was chucking out. At half past three she bought the lot back for ten bob. She couldn't bear to part with a single sock!

Being a Water sign, and ruled by the Moon, Crabs are powerfully psychic, and they will have incredibly intuitive instincts. (When they say they're tuning in, they're not talking about the radio!) Crowds of Cancerians can walk into a room and instantly pick up an atmosphere. (And I don't mean the sultry scent of Saturday's supper – sprouts and stew – either.) Their superb sensitivity also means they can be hurt far too easily, and often over nothing at all. Some of them are hypersensitive, and should realise that when they are told something, it's not always meant as a criticism, or an out-and-out rejection.

Cancerians should try to toughen their soft skins which sit beneath their shells, and not harbour hurts or supposed slights. When they do take umbrage, they become changeable and crabby, mean, moody, huffy and hostile, and almost unapproachable at times. They should use their highly-developed instincts in a positive manner, and trust them and live by them. (Very intense Crabs will tune into their teapots, saying at about four in the afternoon, 'I feel I should put the kettle on.' If you're there, try saying you can sense a custard cream hovering in the biscuit tin.)

Security is of vital importance to Cancerians; often if they feel down and depressed, and are doddering about in the doldrums, it's because they don't have a real base to go home to. They need the emotional security of having their own four walls about them, whereas Taureans need nests for material security.

If you're married to a Cancerian, or have a chum who's a Crab, you have to behave like a cuckoo clock, and at every half hour pop your head round the door and say 'I love you!' (You must mean it, though.) Then they'll feel safe and secure. (Go on, give 'em a kiss!) They can be so gruff that they take you by surprise sometimes. So, if you know a Cancerian who is being crabby, just remember the rocker with the chain mail. (If you're a Bull, you'll remember the crab sandwich!) Underneath that hard shell shimmers a heart of pure gold, which is just waiting to melt as the first words of love cascade from your lips!

Now, of course, there are some cantankerous, cross and cranky Crabs about. They'll be mean and moody, and will scowl like scallops. They'll click away with their pincers, sounding like a couple of castanets on a package holiday, but they will still be soft and sweet underneath.

Cancerians really do need to be needed, and know that they're loved. Otherwise, they can't function fully. Remember this is the polar sign of Capricorn, and most Goats are frightened of rejection. Crabs can be just the same. If they do have particularly firm filial feelings, especially for a matriarchal mum, they'll prefer to hide at home than go out into the big wide world and face whatever it may have to offer them. And when they do scuttle out from under a rock to test the waters of life, if they're used and abused, they'll sound a furious fandango with their perpetually pirouetting pincers, and then rush back to the boulder as fast as their pins can propel them.

Babies are a must for this sign. Whereas procreation is important for Leos, who love children and like to be proud of their own cubs, with Cancer it is much deeper, and more a case of carrying on the family name. Cynthia Crab. Cyril Crab . . .

LEO – 24 JULY–23 AUGUST

Inside every Leo is a king or queen waiting to jump out. (In a little Leo it'll be a prince or princess.) But whatever the rank, Leos do like to wear the crown, hold the sceptre, and be in charge. It's a Leo who will lead a little old lady across the road, even when she doesn't want to go! (You try arguing with a Lion halfway across a zebra crossing!)

Leo's aren't going to like this, but what makes many of them tick is acres of applause. They like to be the centre of attention and know that their public – whether it's 5000 fans or the boy next door – appreciates them.

There are some very colourful Leos around, but there are some very grey ones too. Think of a Leo, and you'll see someone blond and blue-eyed, with a magnificent mane of hair. The men always look like Apollo, who is associated with this sunny sign. And the women are stunningly striking, and have long golden tresses (even if they are out of a bottle!), which shimmer every time they toss their heads in a majestic manner. However, there's another sort, too. This breed look a little like moles, not lions at all, with black barnets, piggy peepers and a rather shifty air! It's very hard to believe that they belong to this splendid sign, but they do!

But whatever they look like, there's no doubt that positive Leos will offer you the earth and give you their hearts. (Gold-plated ones, of course.) There is a gorgeous grandiosity about Leos, but sometimes they can be all mouth. It's only when it's too late that you realise the Lion was just out to impress you.

There was a Lion I used to know, who would offer everyone the earth. He made you feel there was nothing he wouldn't do for you, and promises, offers and assurances flew from his mouth like bees from a hive. The trouble was that those bees never made any honey! It was all hot air, and that's very disappointing indeed from a Lion.

You must never forget (as if the Lions would let you!) that Leo is ruled by the Sun, the centre of the solar system. This star controls almost everything and we'd die without the heat from its rays. So, a lot of Leos can live their lives with a Sun complex. The modest wee beasts feel that as the Sun is the centre of the solar system, so they are centre of the human race!

As a result, of course, they expect people to put down the red carpet for them. Everything has to be done in a stately, stylish way, as if entertaining royalty. When a Leo comes to tea, he or she won't want to be fobbed off with just one fairy cake, but will demand a three-tiered Victoria sponge. This is a regal, dignified and imperial sign, and the Leo will be either an Emperor Nero or Good Queen Bess. But whatever part he or she is playing, it has to be one that doesn't go unnoticed. Leos don't like to be just one of the crowd, like an extra in a scene from *Gone With the Wind*. They want to be Rhett Butler or Scarlett O'Hara. (Lions with strong Cancerian links will want to play Tara, the O'Hara home!)

In astrology, the Sun is our creative core, so Leo is said to be the most creative of the signs. Leos may portray this by playing Annie in *Annie Get Your Gun* at the local amateur dramatic society or by painting their self-portraits on a 40-foot canvas. If they can't be creative themselves in an active way, they'll do it passively, taking off to the theatre or burying themselves in a book. (Why not start with this one?)

Make no mistake, Leo is the sign of the Hollywood musical extravaganza. It may be a bit brash, but it'll have a massive orchestra, and you'll be spellbound by the majesty of it all. And that's what Leos love most. Neptune was tripping the light fantastic through Leo during the great age of Hollywood musicals, which is why they were so lavish. And believe it or not, lots of film producers and directors are Leos – Sam Goldwyn, Alfred Hitchcock, Busby Berkeley and Cecil B. De Mille were all born under this splendid sign of the silver screen. (Leos certainly know how to do things in style.)

There's a fantastic feeling of leisure and pleasure about this sign. Leos love enjoying themselves. (And that's not as obvious as it sounds. Virgos and Capricorns sometimes feel guilty when they have a good knees-up.) They also adore being seen with the right people. (Up-market Leos will be the people the other Leos want to be seen with!)

What makes most Leos tick, though, is very simple. It's the biggest heart imaginable – a sort of titanic ticker. Positive Lions can be wonderfully warm and lastingly loving. And as if that weren't enough, they have a rich sense of humour running through them that will surround you and make you feel safe and secure.

Some Leos aren't lovable Lions at all, but are cheetahs, literally. This sneaky side of the sign comes from the Leonine lust for power. These crafty cats won't have the personality or warmth of the positive Leo, so will have to achieve their ambitions through underhand acts. Don't expect all Leos to want to be centre-stage, because some of them will prefer to wait in the wings, looking on. But most Leos love the limelight, and are happier playing the main man or leading lady. (They may even stick gold stars on their bedroom doors at home.) These Leos aren't concerned with the chorus; they want the bright lights and all that goes with them. Their love of luxury means they can look and dress the part to perfection. But very often they'll behave abominably, and treat everyone as if they were their servants. Don't let a Lion make you his or her skivvy!

Just because a Leo chooses *not* to come on like a Hollywood hotchpotch of Mae West, Cleopatra (don't let her get the needle), and Napoleon Bonaparte, doesn't mean he or she is negative. Sometimes, it's quite the reverse! All you need is a peek at a pirouetting and preening prima donna to see what produces a positive Leo. Some Lions will convey their creative concerto in a quieter, more controlled way. (A Moonlight Sonata rather than an 1812 Overture!) But a positive pussycat will always be the sunshine of your life.

VIRGO – 24 AUGUST–23 SEPTEMBER

Now, before we go any further, think about the Virgos you know. (They're the ones with the neat hairdos and shiny shoes, who make you feel as if you've just been dragged through a hedge backwards.) One of the wonderful things about Virgos is their tremendous talent for organising everything under the sun – starting with themselves. And they really come into their own when they can organise others as well, whether as a cleaning lady or as Home Secretary.

Vestal Virgos of all shapes and sizes are only too pleased to give you a helping hand; their Mercurial motto is 'Service with a smile'. What's more, they really live up to it. You can phone your friend when you're in a fix, and the Virgo will zoom round in ten seconds flat, looking as neat as a new pin. (How do they do it?) If you're feeling as if you've been slung on the scrapheap of life, a Virgo will interrupt your tale of woe with a hundred handy hints and then try to find you another job.

The next thing to remember about this sign is their ceaseless search for perfection. And because they're ruled by Mercury, the planet of the mind and communication, they do this analytically. Geminis spend a lot of time thinking too, but in a swifter, more superficial way. Mercury is more practical in Virgo, restrained by the Earthy element of this sign. This quest for all things perfect means that Virgos don't suffer fools gladly; they like everything to be of the best, both materially and mentally. Sometimes this can go too far, and a Virgo will become fussy and finicky to a fanatical degree. These folk can pick holes in everything, because nothing matches up to their ideals. (But take heart, because the faults they most often find are within themselves.)

Before you've spent five minutes with vestal Virgos you'll have noticed they're naturally neat, and like things to be spick and span, and in apple-pie order. This is the sign of cleanliness, both inner and outer. With most Virgos, this means they just keep everything hunky-dory, but others can go overboard. You'd think they had disinfectant swirling through their systems, they're so obsessed about their health. (A vulnerable Virgoan will moan 'If health is wealth, then I'm broke.')

Now, you may think this sounds a bit much, and that your Virgo pals aren't like that. But they are, even if it's just in a weensy way. Next time you meet a Mercurial mate, listen carefully to the conversation. There'll be at least one reference to keeping clean or tidy, I promise, or you'll hear about their health and hygiene. (This is the sign of hypochondria!) Still not convinced? Well, next time you have a chat in a café with your chum, do a bit of brow-clutching, or seize your stomach and sigh. Say you have a headache, or that you'd better steer clear of the sausage surprise, in case it gives you one later. Your Virgo will come over all concerned, burrow into a bag or briefcase, and produce just the pill guaranteed to get you going again. (They're *that* well organised!)

When it comes to keeping their surroundings sparkling, Virgos beat everyone dusters down. If they visit you, they'll even do your tidying up, not even noticing what they're doing. There was a Virgo girl at school who was invited to more parties then all the debs in Devon, because her idea of a good time was frolicking with the

Fairy Liquid in the kitchen. Put your shandy down for a second and she'd have whizzed in and whisked it away, then given the glass a good going-over in the suds in the sink. (Invite a few Virgos to your next knees-up, and you won't even have to clear away a cup – it'll all be done for you! But you've got to pick the right sort, because some of them are unutterably untidy.)

Because Virgos are usually tidy-minded and orderly, they can be somewhat sceptical and suspicious of anything they don't understand. For them, seeing is believing: they're innately inquisitive, and like to find things out for themselves. That means it's hard to pull the wool over their eyes, because they can see straight through any fast-talking. Anyone who's a fly-by-night won't stand a chance once those Mercurial minds get moving.

Virgos who make the most of their mental mastery and organisational ability can go a long way at work. (And I don't mean they make lovely long-distance lorry drivers, either!) But you might not hear about that almost certain success. Virgos are very modest, and hate blowing their own trumpets. Even when they win accolades and awards they'll prefer to keep quiet.

Unfortunately, Virgos sometimes carry this ravishing reticence into other areas of their lives. Not only will they be coy professionally, but they'll be retiring romantically, too. Their heads usually rule their hearts and Virgos can be quite cool, undemonstrative and unemotional. One Virgo relative of mine married purely for tax reasons.

This is definitely a sign that finds it hard to slow down, and Mercury makes Virgos move about like maniacs – busy bees! They can have dreadful difficulties relaxing, and will always find something to do, even if it's the dusting – for the third time in a morning. Which reminds me. I was chatting to a Mercurial male one day, and we were discussing what he'd done during Christmas. He said his girlfriend had gone to Glasgow, and left him at home. Did he mind? 'Oh no!' he grinned. 'It meant I could tidy up my flat. And I got the tops of the plugs clean. It was wonderful!' Obviously he got thirteen amps of joy from Santa that Christmas!

LIBRA – 24 SEPTEMBER–23 OCTOBER

Sugar and spice and all things nice – that's what Librans are made of. Even if you get the rare one made from puppy-dogs' tails, you can bet they'll be pretty pooches and handsome hounds. So it may come as a shock to you that this sweet, sublime sign is the iron hand in the velvet glove. 'What? Our Ethel?' I can hear you saying, but read on, my dears. Libra is a Cardinal Air sign, which means that Librans know what they want, and usually have the mental mastery to be able to get it. I mean, look at Margaret Thatcher!

Libra's ruling planet is Venus, which makes subjects of this sign courteous, charming, cheerful, caring, caressable and captivatingly cuddly. Make no mistake, loquacious Librans can charm the birdies right out of the trees when they want to. (And scintillate the squirrels while they're about it.) But if you look closely, they usually have an aim for all that charm and diplomacy.

Take a woman who has the Sun, Moon, Mars and Jupiter all in luscious Libra. (Gosh!) One day she discovered that a near-neighbour didn't give two hoots about her so she moved heaven and earth until she did, but she killed her with kindness in the process! (And piqued all her pals, who felt ignored.)

The trouble is that Librans like to be liked. In fact, they can't bear to believe that someone can't stand them. Venus can bestow beauteous bounty on her boys and girls, but sometimes she can make them too sweet for words. Even when a Libran is at his or her sugariest and sickliest, you must work out what's behind it all. Librans are assertive, ambitious and go-ahead. So they always have an end in sight. (*Votre derrière*, dear.) It could be to keep the peace (incredibly important to Librans), or to get a new job, but it will be something. Of the other Cardinal signs, Ariens will tramp through the rest of the zodiac, Cancerians will drown everyone in tears, and Capricorns will lumber along like a ten-ton tank. But Librans try to get what they want with a smile. (And they usually succeed.)

This is the sign of nuptial bliss, of partnerships of all persuasions, both in business and in love. (Committed relationships of one sort or another loom large in a Libran life.) And so it's the sign of enemies, too. After all, you can have a rapport with a rival just as much as you'll have an affinity with an amourette. The strength of the emotion is the same. Although the Libran motto is 'Peace at all costs', you mustn't forget the razor's edge between love and hate.

The polar sign of Libra is Aries, and these two can have a wonderful relationship, because they balance each other beautifully. (And remember that though Librans, being the sign of the Scales, are always trying to achieve perfect harmony in their lives, their own set of scales can go up and down like yo-yos.) The archetypal Arien-Libran relationship is the Tarzan and Jane jamboree. There's Arien Tarzan swinging through the shrubbery, leaping about in a little loincloth, while Libran Jane stays at home being perky and pretty, probably with a little dishcloth. (Wearing it, of course, in a lovely shade of pink.) The Libran's keyword is 'You', whereas Ariens say '*Me!*'. Librans can think too much of their partners and pals, to their own detriment, and can stride off through sleet and snow to minister to a mate who's ill. Some of them can be too selfless for words, although they may still be doing it for a reason – to be liked and loved!

Librans should stop being so concerned with the welfare of their loved ones, and think of themselves sometimes instead. In astrology, every sign has a positive and a negative side, and if you go to extremes in either direction it can be terrible.

This is the sign of puffy pink clouds, baby-blue angora wool and pink-and-white icing. You see, Libra is a very pretty sign indeed. It's not as fantastical and fairy-tale as the Fish, because Librans have more of a sense of reality. Nevertheless, the Libran quest is very much for beauty, and with this love for all things bright and beautiful, Librans can't cope with anything coarse, callous or crude.

The trouble with Librans is that they can be irritatingly inde-cisive; you can go grey while waiting for them to make up their minds about whether to feast on a fairy cake or have a blow-out on bangers and mash. (In the end you want to bash them over the bonce with the frying pan.) That may be why they're so considerate, and always ask you what *you* want to do, what *you* want to eat – because they know they haven't the foggiest idea. (Although lots of them *do* know, and try to coerce you into choosing their choice.)

They also like to keep everything fair and square, and if they feel they've been wronged, they'll fight like Aries or be as stubborn as the most intransigent Taurean to prove they're in the right. Justice must be seen to be done – in the Libran's eyes, at least. (Negative Librans will get their sense of justice a mite mixed up.) But even positive Librans will tamper with the balance they find in their lives, on their oh-so-sensitive scales, and wonder if they've got it right. ('On the other hand,' they'll sigh, 'I could be wrong.' This sort of soul-searching can go on for ever, and frequently does!)

Librans' love of harmony and balance extends to matters of the heart, as you might expect. They must have luscious lovers (they must be physically fantastic), and the Libran man must have the most beautiful bird in town in tow, even if he's as ugly as a vulture himself (though he'll have a smashing smile and delicious dimples). Accuse Librans of this and they will say in a superior way that they're an intellectual Air sign, and so plump for personality, first and foremost. But you try to get a Libran to go out with someone who's no oil painting, but has bags of bounce and bonhomie, and see what happens. That's right. *Nothing!*

SCORPIO – 24 OCTOBER–22 NOVEMBER

Listen. Do you want to know a secret? (Where have I heard that line before?) Do you promise not to tell? Scorpios are ace! Their coolness can be captivating, and their furtiveness fascinating. And they're so laid-back it's luscious!

Scorpios have more undercurrents than a conger eel. You never know what makes them tick because they never give you a clue. (Is it clockwork or quartz?) They sit looking enigmatic, and you wonder what on earth they're thinking about!

In fact, enigmatic is the supreme Scorpio word. The normal give-away for this Plutonic sign is the eyes, which are like deep pools – you wonder what's going on below the surface. Scorpios are like icebergs; after all, if you combine their element, Water, with their Fixed quality, what do you get but ice?

Aries and Scorpio share the ancient rulership of mighty Mars, yet their temperaments are as different as chalk and cheese. Ariens have flashes of Fiery fury, and act on impulse (they'll suddenly strangle you with a sock). Scorpios, though, simmer and smoulder on the back burner of life's cooker, plotting and planning how to get even with you. And they'll manage it in the end! Scorpios have psychological power, and use it to the full whenever they can. (They could manipulate Machiavelli!)

Never underestimate a Scorpio. This is a phantasmagorically profound placing for a person, and Scorpios are imbued with intensity. This is, after all, the sign of sex and death.

Death, for a Scorpio, isn't always something physical; instead these folk can kill off certain sections of their lives they no longer like in the twinkling of an eye. They can transform and transfigure their lives more than any other sign, making fresh starts with barely a backward glance. However, since this is the sign of obsessions, some Scorpios are fascinated by physical death, and can gad about graveyards, looking at the headstones and absorbing the atmosphere. They'll be engrossed and enthralled by the ritual of death, and almost have death wishes, because they can't wait to know what it's like on the other side. Other Scorpios go to the opposite extreme, and are petrified of popping off!

Make no mistake, this is a sign of such compulsion, obsession and profundity that some people find Scorpios hard to handle. Just thinking about their intense inquisitions, interrogations and investigations makes some folk's hair stand on end! Scorpios can be like an oil rig, drilling deep into the heart of the matter. (I wonder how many of the men are called Derrick?) And if you want to know what makes a Scorpio tick, you've got to do the same to them. Then you'll start to see what's submerged beneath that superficially serene surface. (A Scorpio may come across as cool, calm and collected, but underneath that elegant exterior is a sizzling selection of scorching sensations simply seething away!)

Power is very important to these Plutonians, but it's always gained in a secretive way. Scorpios operate behind the scenes; they love to manipulate others, but hate to be caught in the glare of the spotlight themselves.

But don't just think there's only one sort of Scorpio, who's like the Spanish Inquisition. There are three sides to the sign, from the angelic to the awful. Top of the list is the devout Dove. This is the Scorpio who believes in peace and tranquillity, and strives for it at all costs. (Perhaps even becoming a nun or a monk in the process.) Next comes the exciting Eagle – the daredevil hero who takes risks and laughs in the face of danger. Whether James or Jane Bond, this Scorpio works behind the scenes as a spy or a secret agent. (You can always spot 'em because they shin up drainpipes in the dark, clutching cartons of chocs between their teeth!) So far so good, I hear you say. But lastly comes the sly Snake, that slithers through the undergrowth of life, then slinks out when you least expect it, and buries its fangs in your ankle. Ouch! These are the mass-murderers, the Charles Mansons of the world. (No wonder Scorpios can get a bad name!)

Luckily for the rest of us, that is the lowest level to which a Scorpio can sink. (It's the lowest level to which anyone can sink!) Higher-minded Scorpios choose to follow a positive path, seeking out the spiritual side of life. But a truly negative Scorpio will turn to black magic to fulfil that pulverising passion for power, taking a macabre interest in things most people shy away from. Once you've totally understood a complex Scorpio you'll have solved one of astrology's most ancient mysteries, and be shown sensational sights of life that no other sign can offer.

SAGITTARIUS – 23 NOVEMBER–21 DECEMBER

Talk about clumsy! If Sagittarians aren't putting both feet in it verbally, they're doing it physically, and landing up to their necks in trouble. If you ask an Archer round for afternoon tea, don't get out the best china. It'll only get broken. (Use some plastic plates instead.) Your Sagittarian pal will rush into the room and trip over the tea table, sending the cups and saucers flying in all directions. Then, to add insult to injury, as your mate dashes off for a dishcloth to mop up the mess, he or she will step on a cream cake and crunch it into the carpet. Still, having your residence wrecked is often better than hearing the truth about yourself, Sagittarian style. Your friend can say 'I saw someone who looked just like you yesterday.' However, before you feel pleased, and start to preen, wait for the punchline. 'Then I realised it was someone else, because you've got more spots.' See what I mean?

But let's look on the bright side – something that's second nature to our jovial pals. Sagittarians are incurable optimists (their beer bottles are always half full, never half empty), and they will inject others with their infectious enthusiasm, given half a chance. If you're feeling really down in the dumps, your Sagittarian pal will bounce up, tell you a joke or two and try to get you giggling again. Go on, give 'em a grin! Jupiter, the planet that rules these Archers, makes them magnificently merry, and they'll try to jolly everyone else along too. The terrific thing about them is that they usually succeed. You can't mooch about moping for long when there's an Archer around.

Because this is the polar sign of garrulous Gemini, Sagittarians are also blessed with the gift of the gab, and can talk the hind leg off a donkey. But there is a mighty difference between these two signs. Astrologically, Gemini is the lower-minded sign, dealing with subjects superficially and knowing a little about a lot, while Sagittarius is the opposite, full of philosophy and worldly wisdoms. (In ancient mythology, the Centaur – the Sagittarius symbol – was the master of teaching and healing.) During a deep discussion with an Archer, you'll find that they're searching for the meaning of life, and will ponder on the problem all through their existence. ('What's it all about, Alfie?' is definitely the Sagittarian song!) Faiths and beliefs are all-important to Archers.

Now, it's not for nothing that Sagittarius is the sign of the Archer. There's the hunter, poised with his bow and arrow, all a-quiver, taking aim at a target. Archers do this throughout their lives (always aiming for the bull's-eye), but the trouble is they often aim too high, and miss the target by miles. They set their sights too high (literally!). Sometimes, of course, an Archer will get it right first time, but usually life to these folk is like a rerun of the Battle of Hastings, with arrows flying in all directions. (If you're called Harold, you should head for the hills!)

It's all gigantic Jupiter's doing. Because he's the largest planet in the heavens, he gives some of these Sagittarians ideas above their stations. This can be a terrific trait, because it means that the Sagittarian is always striving for better things. But some Centaurs can go to the opposite extreme and exaggerate everything they come into contact with. As a result, they get everything out of proportion; they bounce about, blowing their own bugles, believing the world can't turn without them. You see, Jupiter knows no bounds – and neither do Sagittarians. (The world doesn't just end at Ambridge for these Archers!)

This is the universal sign, and all Archers are tantalised by travel and the thought of far-flung corners of the globe. Think of the Sagittarians you know. You'll find that lots of them went round the world as soon as they could, or lived in a foreign country at some point in their lives. (Their passports contain more stamps than a Stanley Gibbons catalogue!) This desire to get out and see the world for themselves can be the making of positive Sagittarians. Negative Archers, though, can wax lyrical about their exotic adventures, name-dropping like mad, so it sounds as though they spent a weekend at the White House, when actually they only whizzed past it on a bus.

Jupiter is the planet of luck and opportunity, and some Archers are just like cats, with nine lives. (Some of them are so accident-prone, they need all the help they can get!) You may think they're gauche and rude, but they call it being honest! They make the most of every opportunity that arises, and can often spot a chance when others don't think it's there. Sometimes that'll be their brilliant perception and vision, and other times it'll be blind faith and living in cloud-cuckoo-land. It's up to the Archer to decipher the mystical Morse code.

Meet a positive Sagittarian and you will be fulfilled in many ways, and imbued with a zest and a zeal for living. But a negative Archer can be crafty, or will let you down in some way or other, whether emotionally or materially. These folk can waste everyone's time, and will bite off more than they can chew. All Sagittarians need challenges; they need to know where to aim their celestial bows and arrows so they can hit the target fair and square. After all, it's much better to climb the ladder of life, rung by rung, than to take a flying leap at it and miss by miles!

CAPRICORN – 22 DECEMBER–20 JANUARY

Right, repeat after me, 'Capricorns are captivating.' Say it again. Got it? Good. Now remember it, and forget what you might have heard about these folk being morose and melancholic. You will find some Goats with a grouse, because there are positive and negative folks in every sign, but a together Goat can be gorgeous.

Let's get the worst over first with this sign. Some Capricorns can be the original wet blankets, moaning and misanthropic, complaining and carping, and generally being gloomy old things. You'll look at them and think 'I don't want to know you.' But if you bother to get to know them, you can have the time of your life. Talk about giggle!

One of the tremendous traits of this bunch is their superb sense of humour and wit that's as dry as a bone, but much more fun. They can take the mickey out of everything – including themselves, which makes them very endearing indeed. And they really do act the goat, making you laugh until your sides split. Once you've glimpsed the sensational side of this sign, you can turn a blind eye to its more *triste* traits, because you'll have found the silver lining to the Capricorn cloud. (And the crock of gold at the end of the rainbow, if the Goat has Taurus rising.)

Some negative Capricorns can pick holes in everything – even if they hit the jackpot at bingo, they'll moan about having to spend all that money. The poor things can't express their emotions, either, and will bottle up all their feelings and frustrations.

When you meet a Capricorn, expect them to act older than their years. Goats age in the opposite way to the rest of us, behaving as if they were fifty when they're only five, and seven when they're seventy. This means that Capricorns make elderly-seeming babies and young-at-heart pensioners. When the rest of us are being put out to grass, Goats are just coming into their own!

This is a sign that believes in experience, with a capital 'E'. They never have an easy life until they've blown out all the candles on their thirtieth birthday cakes. Until then, life will have been one long struggle; the only way for them to survive is to learn by experience. (Capricorns hate wasting *anything*!) Many of them will have had cramped childhoods, awful adolescences and terrible twenties. But they'll have terrific thirties, fantastic forties – even naughty nineties!

There are two types of Goat – the ones who cavort and curvet up the crags to the summit of their own mountainsides, and the ones who are domestic, and like to potter about their own pieces of pasture, never straying far from the fireside. Capricorns are Cardinal, making them astoundingly ambitious, and even the domestic ones will be determined to do well. Success for them, though, isn't totally based on boodle (although they'd never refuse owt for nowt!); honour, public position and status all smell sweet to them.

Capricorns need security, which they get from the tried, true and tested. They love history, and anything with a past (this could mean you), because then they feel safe. Capricorns are conservative, canny and cautious, and are suspicious of new-fangled things, until they get used to them. They hate to fly in the face of convention.

They're very wary of wearing out their wallets, too. They believe that if they take care of the farthings, the pennies will look after themselves. More positive Goats would call themselves careful, and will be generous with their loot when they've got it, and laugh about it when they haven't. (Always with a note of caution in their grin!)

Guilt is a very Goaty thing, and some Capricorns thrive on it, putting everyone through the mill, including themselves. They can set themselves impossibly high ideals, and almost galactic goals, and then hate themselves when they fail to reach them. Because just as they hate waste, they also can't abide failure. (It's a good job they're imbued with endurance and endeavour!) They are deeply determined and disciplined, so can drive themselves to hit heights others only dream of.

But not all Goats are quite so positive. Some delight in the doldrums, like grumpy old Eeyore in *Winnie the Pooh* – a donkey who's always down in the dumps. But still everyone adored him. In fact, with a little understanding, you are sure to have fun with even the most morose Goats: laugh with them, but never at them, and you'll never feel down!

AQUARIUS – 21 JANUARY–19 FEBRUARY

You learn a whole new vocabulary when you meet an Aquarian. Forget about the usual words, and ponder on ones like 'contrary', 'bizarre', 'radical' and 'outrageous'. In fact, you'd do well to remember them, because you're going to need them.

Before I go any further, let's get one thing straight. Well, two if you're going to be pedantic. (And if you are, make sure it's not in front of an Aquarian. They aren't particularly pleased by pedantic people.) There are two types of Aquarians: those ruled by Saturn and those ruled by Uranus. It's strange, I know, but then a lot of people think Aquarians are strange . . . (Watch it, because I'm one of them.)

Saturn is the ancient ruler of Aquarius; when rebellious, revolutionary Uranus was revealed he was given to the Sun sign most fitting that description – Airy Aquarius. (Some people think Aquarius is a Water sign, but it isn't. Its symbol may be the Water Carrier, but it is actually the third of the Air signs. Confusing, isn't it?)

Saturn Aquarians tend to be conservative, reliable and positive pillars of proper society. You won't catch them wearing lampshades for hats, unless you've spiked their sherry. If that sounds a bit like Capricorn, you're right. Saturn Aquarians do have a lot of Capricorn's characteristics, so if you think you know one, turn back to the previous chapter and have a gander at the Goats.

I'm going to deal mostly with Uranus-ruled Aquarians here. (Usually, you will discover which planet is strongest by studying the birth chart. Sometimes it will be easier – you may meet an Aquarian who is so Saturnine it's not true, or so unusual that they have to be Uranian. Unless they're just plain mad.)

An ancient astrological adage says you can't tell Aquarians anything because they know it already, and very often will tell you so. One of the negative qualities of Aquarians is their one-upmanship. You can meet an Aquarian mate for a meal, and arrive in a wheelchair with your bonce in a big bandage. As the waiter whizzes you to the table, you will smile through your layers of lint, expecting a sudden show of sympathy. The Aquarian will look up, and ask you what happened. So far so good. After you've mumbled in a muffled manner that you were weeding your window box and fell off, fracturing your femur and splitting your skull, the Aquarian will sigh, say 'Oh, is that all?' and go on to recount how they once broke both arms *and* both legs, wrecked their ribs and biffed their back, while morris dancing at Kew Gardens. It can make you mad, but don't kick them with your cast, because it'll hurt you more than them. The negative Saturn Aquarian can be like the negative Capricorn, and be plagued with pessimism, downcast by depression and doubt, and worn out with worry.

The two halves of Aquarius are so very different. If the Saturn type is black and white, then the Uranian Aquarian is all the colours in the spectrum. They can be completely confusing, contrary, unpredictable and incomprehensible – qualities that set them completely apart from their Saturn brothers and sisters. Uranus Aquarians are all of a jitter, rushing here and there, and constantly changing their moods. They remind me of Merlin, popping up when you least expect it. In astrology, Uranus is known as the great awakener, as if a magic wand had been waved, the word 'abracadabra' said. He will create change in something that was static. So, the Uranus-ruled Aquarian is ceaselessly craving change.

On a positive level, this means that the Aquarian is eternally excited and exhilarated by what may lie round the corner, and there may be sudden changes of career, luck or partners when Uranus decides to stage a shake-up. Negatively, an Aquarian will want to change things just for the sake of it, because he or she longs to rock the boat. Routine can be anathema to an Aquarian; the Saturn Aquarian, on the other hand, may find it rather reassuring. This is the quintessence of the Aquarian quandary – complete contradiction, with one half of the sign panting for pastures new, and the other following the furrow.

You never know what's going to happen next with an Aquarian. Life can be a lot of fun, or you can find it very tiring. Aquarians are unconventional, but they are also original, and along with Geminis, are said to be the geniuses of the zodiac. They can be inventive and brilliantly clever, although sometimes they are spectacular in such a strange way, so abstract and off at such a tremendous tangent, that no one knows what they're talking about! Aquarians are really born way ahead of their time. (After all, they laughed at Christopher

Columbus when he said the world was round!) Other people, who are rather less free-thinking and original, will conclude that they are completely cranky.

Another Aquarian contradiction is that although Water Carriers are said to be humanitarians, they can be emotional ice cubes in the cocktail of life, and don't easily express their emotions. They *can* be humanitarian – helping others, sending cash to charities, or being affectionate on a large scale – yet find their own close relationships difficult to cope with. Aquarius is a Fixed sign, so it can be intolerably inflexible and intransigent. For all their brainpower and brilliance, Aquarians can be staggeringly stupid and stubborn, standing their ground over a long-lost cause and unable to admit they are in the wrong.

Since Aquarius is an Air sign, the Aquarian will be much more mesmerised by a marriage of the minds than a partnership of passion and physical fulfilment. Very often, they pick the most unlikely-looking person for a partner, because they will have chosen them for their mind rather than for anything else. Aquarians can have some very avant-garde relationships! (Ever heard of Beauty and the beast? And guess who's playing Beauty!)

Aquarians think of the future a great deal; often when they have just crossed one hurdle, they will think 'Where will this lead?' and 'I wonder what's going to happen next?' And this brings me to another Aquarian attribute. They are the only sign to answer a question with a question. Ask an Aquarian if it's raining, and he or she will ask you why you want to know. (A Piscean would say yes, and offer to lend you their green gamp.) The first word Aquarian children learn is 'Why?', and they will continue to ask that question all through their lives.

You can never get really close to an Aquarian. Unless they have plenty of Pisces and Taurus in their charts to warm them up, they can be aloof and cold and difficult to cuddle. But for all that, life with an Aquarian, either as a pal or a partner, will never be dull, and that's something to think about!

PISCES – 20 FEBRUARY–20 MARCH

Saintly Pisces! Some of these Fish should be canonised, they are so far advanced along the road to spiritual enlightenment. (Others still seem to be waiting at the heavenly bus stop!)

Now, there are two sorts of Pisceans; this last sign of the zodiac is ruled by two planets – jocular, jaunty Jupiter, and nebulous, nectarine Neptune. The Jupiter-ruled Pisceans are very akin to Sagittarians, because they share the same ruler. But Jupiterian Pisceans aren't prone to the flights of fancy shown by Sagittarians. Their ruler represents wealth and good fortune, and the Jupiterian Fish will always have an eye on these things. In fact, Pisces brings out these Jupiterian qualities beautifully, making the Fish full of fun and clever at bringing in the boodle. Negatively, there will be a tendency towards overexpansion, whether in girth, mirth, or wheeling and dealing. But these Jupiterian Fish do burst with bounteous bonhomie, and can be gloriously generous and marvellously magnanimous.

Because of the saintly side of this sign, Pisceans can be very devout and pious. (It depends on the Fish whether that will make you awed or bored.) If they are ruled by Jupiter, they will accept the faith or religion they have been brought up in. A Neptunian Piscean, however, will be more unusual, even mystical, and may find Eastern religions especially attractive.

This is a profoundly psychic sign, and the Piscean should use this ability positively to live a better life. Many Fish become fascinated by black magic and the occult, like Scorpios, because they are seduced by secrecy. But, generally, Pisceans have an inspiration that can draw them wholeheartedly into the realms of the positive supernatural and mystical. They are also intensely interested in spiritualism, because it helps them to get in touch with that unseen lot they feel so much a part of.

Neptunian Pisceans waft along on clouds, daydreaming away to their heart's content. They really aren't part of this world at all! (This isn't the same as Aquarians, who are futuristic, and one step ahead of everyone else. Pisceans are unworldly in a filigree, fantasial way.) These Fish will appear magical and mystical, and they can be profoundly artistic and unworldly sometimes, to the point of being gullible or geniuses. Lord Byron had powerful Piscean placings, and Mozart and Chopin both had the Sun in this sign, as does Rudolph Nureyev, who brought a whole new concept to ballet. (And to tights. Pisceans love to leave something to the imagination!)

What you must remember about Neptune is that this planet gives an illusory image to everything it encounters. Neptune represents something that can never be captured or held on to. Think of an intangible will-o'-the-wisp, or a piece of thistledown floating through the air that always eludes you, and you have the perfect picture of Pisceans.

They can bring this quality into their everyday lives, imbuing them with illusion, and smothering them in strange sea mists. You will think you're looking at one thing, then the shadows shift and you discover you're seeing something quite different.

Everything that Neptune does is intensified in an ethereal way, so Neptunian Pisceans will be hypersensitive, and as fragile as a butterfly's wing. They can feel neurotically nauseated by anything ugly, whether it's society, sights, sounds or situations. Some Fishy folk can't stand the slightest facial flaw, let alone anything else. (Better talk to them with your head hidden!) Yet such is their spiritual self-awareness, that often they will devote their lives to the very vocations which you'd think they couldn't bear. For example, they might join the prison service (but not behind bars!), look after the old and infirm, and the mentally and physically handicapped. These positive Pisceans force themselves to face up to their phobias, and bring some good out of them. (Other Pisceans will only want the erotic, exotic, seductive and sumptuous side of life, and none of the unpleasant parts.)

I can hear you saying 'That sounds like Libra!', and you'd be right. Neptune is said to be the higher octave of Venus, a sort of top C of the zodiac. It's like a dog whistle, which has a note that's too high for humans to hear. And this is what Neptunian natives are like – they're listening to a high-pitched tone that the rest of us can't catch. Equally, Jupiter is said to be the higher octave of Mercury, and Jupiterian folk can understand all the deeper things of life that a Mercury-ruled person skims over. Between them, Mercury and Jupiter rule the four Mutable signs – Gemini, Virgo, Sagittarius and Pisces. (Interesting, isn't it?).

Neptune is a fantastically fantasial figure. On a positive level, its influence means that Neptunians can be wonderful writers, divine dancers and profound poets. (And incurable romantics.) But negatively, they can be monstrously Machiavellian, playing one person off against another. Some of them make Lucretia Borgia look like Little Bo Peep; they can be malicious and malevolent, vicious and venomous, treacherous and two-faced. (They have a wonderful way of believing their own fibs and fables.) And this is how we get the symbol of Pisces, which is a fish swimming in different directions. Pisceans are either way up at the top of the tree or at rock bottom; either the nurse helping the drug addict or the addict himself.

Fish are vulnerable, and can be victims of the unknown, murky depths of their imaginations and subconscious minds. They are either inspired, or they're the dregs of the earth, who rely on society to look after them.

There's no getting away from it. This sign is a mystery, but not in a Scorpionic way. Rather, it's unworldly, in a delicious, delectable, gossamer-like way. There is a floaty, flimsy veil hiding what is really going on in the Piscean life. The Fish can inhabit a very weird world, and the worst thing Pisceans can do is to drift along on an aimless sea, when their phobias, fetishes and fixations may well get the better of them. They are very impressionable indeed, and negative Pisceans will be plagued by psychosomatic problems that they have brought on themselves. Positive Pisceans can direct that abundant artistry, that magnificent mysticism, into a brilliant conclusion. Or they can live such serene spiritual lives that nothing else matters, because their tremendous inner peace brings them total fulfilment.

Think of your Fishy friends, and you'll realise that something strange sets them apart from everyone else. You can't put your finger on it, but you know it's there. Remember those sea mists. One minute the view is as clear as a bell, the next you're sinking into a ferocious fog! It's a magical, mystical mystery.

RUSSELL'S RELATIONSHIP GUIDE

TAURUS MAN AND ARIES WOMAN

Smashing! What a contented couple you two can be, especially if you've fallen for the sort of Ramette who rushes around from dawn to dusk. You may not join in, but you'll always enjoy watching your Arien amour being so energetic! Let's face it, you like to live your lives at very different paces, and you two can be like the tortoise and the hare. All the same, if you can find a compromise, then you'll have a lot to smile about. If you're a Taurean chap worth his salt, the fun-loving ways of your vivacious, vital and vivid Arien lass will soon have you eating out of her hand and showering her with presents, gifts and lots of lovely luxuries. Sexually speaking, you're the tops together, and can enjoy some delectably tactile, sensual and steamy interludes!

TAURUS MAN AND TAURUS WOMAN

Delicious, delightful and de-lovely – that's the only way to describe it when two Taureans start waltzing hand in hand through the dance hall of life. You're both happiest when you're having a cosy, comfy and cosseted existence, so you'll spoil each other rotten – especially when it comes to eating yourselves out of house and home! Sexually you're on exactly the same wavelength, and even if you do only know one tune in the sexual hit parade (you don't like trying out anything new), you'll play it again and again! The only cloud on the horizon could crop up when you fall out with each other, as you're both so stubborn and obstinate that neither of you will admit you're in the wrong. You could also be stick-in-the-muds when it comes to trying out anything new, but the fixity that makes you stand your ground will mean that you're loyal lovers from first to last, sticking together through thick and thin.

TAURUS MAN AND GEMINI WOMAN

Will you or won't you? It's one of those relationships that could go with a swing or soon hit snarls and snags. You see, you both have such different desires and outlooks on life that you may be poles apart. If you both share the same idea of fun then life will be much easier, but if you're the sort of boy Bull who likes to know exactly what his amourette is up to, then you're going to find yourself in a pretty pickle when it comes to keeping track of your Gemini girl. After all, she hates being tied down by anything or anyone and won't take kindly to your questions about where she's been and what she's been doing. There could also be problems in the passion stakes, as you adore having kisses and cuddles and your Mercurial miss may not like that one bit! If you want to keep her happy you'll have to mix some words with your actions.

TAURUS MAN AND CANCER WOMAN

How touching! It's a delight to see you two together, because it's a partnership made in heaven. Cosy companionship is what you both need, and you'll support each other come what may. You make fantastic friends but even more splendid sweethearts or spouses, and as the years go by you'll be drawn even closer together. For a lady Crab, it's second nature to look after her amour, especially if that means spending hours in the kitchen concocting magnificent meals and scrumptious snacks, and you'll be delighted to put them all to the Taurean taste test and help her to scoff the lot! The only thing to suffer will be your waistlines! Best of all, you'll feel safe and secure with your Cancerian amour, knowing that you both value fidelity and loyalty above all else. What a contented couple!

TAURUS MAN AND LEO WOMAN

We shall not moved – that's your theme song when you pair up with a Leo lady. Because you're both Fixed signs of the zodiac, you believe in standing your ground and sticking to your guns whenever there's a disagreement or discussion. Neither of you likes giving in or admitting you might be wrong, which can lead to lots of stormy scenes and tempestuous tirades! There can also be some pretty sultry scenarios whenever you bourré off to the bedroom, and your Taurean passion combines with your Leo lass's gift for amour. What a captivating combination! However, if you believe that a woman's place is in the home, you could hit big trouble when you team up with this pretty pussycat, as she prefers to be out on the town or having a smashing spending spree with your loot. Unless you want to fall out fast, then why not grin and bear it, and join in the fun?

TAURUS MAN AND VIRGO WOMAN

Are you prepared for some hard work? The more effort the two of you can put into this relationship, the better it'll be. Take each other at face value, though, and you'll never discover the prodigious potential of this pairing, whether sexually, emotionally or platonically, and that would be a waste! You see, you may both be Earth signs, but that's where the resemblance ends. As a Bull, you like to know that everything will stay the same, no matter what, whereas your Virgo valentine adores all the variety and change that life has to offer. Once you're together, you'll love the way your vestal Virgo makes your abode look as pretty as a picture, and she'll adore knowing that she can depend on you come what may. Learn to understand and appreciate each other's needs, and you'll be glad you made the effort.

TAURUS MAN AND LIBRA WOMAN

Love truly is a many-splendoured thing when you fall for a Libran lass. In fact, it can be heaven on earth, thanks to your shared ruler, velvety and voluptuous Venus. Her ravishing rays transform you into a tremendously tactile Taurean, always wanting to cuddle and caress your amorous and affectionate Libran love. That way you both get what you want! (You could be hot stuff for her at first, but she'll soon get used to it!) What's more, because you're one of the Fixed folk of the zodiac, you're the soul of fidelity and loyalty, and totally trustworthy – perfect for your Venusian miss who's spent her life looking for the knight in shining amour who'll whisk her off her feet and never let her down! She'll revel in your aura of sophistication and romance, and luxuriate in your love of the good life. What a divine duo!

TAURUS MAN AND SCORPIO WOMAN

Passion personified! That's what you get when you fall head over heels for a Scorpio dame, and you're almost certain to be a very earthy, sexy and carnal couple. After all, you're ruled by the planet of love and she belongs to the sexiest sign of all, so you're bound to have hours of fun in the boudoir, bathroom, back garden and anywhere else that your fancy takes you! (It'll be Firework Night every evening for you two!) Being faithful to each other goes without saying and you'd be deeply disappointed if your partner wasn't a wee bit possessive and jealous every now and then. Let's face it, you need to own each other body and soul. Even so, make sure you've got separate interests or your set-up will get stale, stagnant and stifling. What a waste that would be!

TAURUS MAN AND SAGITTARIUS WOMAN

In astrology, no combination of signs is wrong, but some are more difficult to cope with than others – and, guess what, this is one of them! You see, you really do look at life from opposite ends of the spectrum. As a pragmatic and practical Bull, you don't like taking even the smallest risks, whereas your Archerette adores aiming for the stars. It can be enough to drive you to distraction, especially if she's using your hard-earned cash to finance all her schemes and dreams, which you think are just pie in the sky. Exotic and erotic encounters can be another problem, as she may find your pulsating passions too hot to handle whilst you accuse her of being as cool as a cucumber, or even of thinking about something completely different! You've got to talk out your differences and find a happy medium, or your relationship could be over almost as soon as it's begun.

TAURUS MAN AND CAPRICORN WOMAN

Money talks when you two get together. In fact, it speaks volumes! You're both very concerned about cash, and once you've discovered that you both think along the same lines moneywise, with no danger that one of you will run off with the proceeds of the piggy bank or joint account, then you'll be in clover. (You've got to get your priorities right!) As you're both Earth signs, there's a deliciously sensual and seductive feel to all amorous encounters that will keep you both happy and content, and you'll bring out all sorts of sensations and sentiments that neither of you knew about.

You're just as good in the boardroom as the bedroom, 'cos you make brill business partners, with you able to keep a firm grip on the boodle and your Goaty girl good at masterminding the whole operation. Your perfect pairing can lead to prestige and profit as well as passion, and you can't say fairer than that!

TAURUS MAN AND AQUARIUS WOMAN

If you're the sort of boy Bull who won't budge over issues, then you've more than met your match when you team up with an Aquarian lass. You're both past masters at standing your ground and refusing to alter your opinions, but unless you can both learn to compromise you'll never get anywhere. Let's face it, you won't agree on anything, whether it's what time to have your tea or where to go for your holidays! This could be a very problematic pairing indeed, especially if you're both intransigent, intractable and downright bloody-minded! Your Aquarian dame may also think you're too bovine and boring for words, whilst you find her outré and outrageous ways a wee bit frightening or intimidating. Make no mistake, this relationship will never be plain sailing, but you're both such strong characters that maybe that's the very thing that'll keep you together!

TAURUS MAN AND PISCES WOMAN

Luscious and loving, this is a liaison that'll warm the cockles of your huge hearts. You're like kindred spirits once you get together, especially where your emotions are concerned. You'll revel in the powerful, protective and passionate feelings that your sensitive wee female Fish arouses in you, and you'll delight in her dainty and doting ways. An air of refinement and sophistication will make your abode somewhere very special indeed as you both give vent to your tremendous potential and get involved in all sorts of artistic ventures. Another way of using your creativity is when it comes to intimate affairs, as you'll both play every sexy game under the sun and live out your Fish's fantasies to the hilt. Just remember that variety is the spice of life, 'cos if you let your loving run into a rut, your pretty Piscean may decide to get her Cupidic kicks elsewhere . . .

TAURUS WOMAN AND ARIES MAN

Compromise needs to be the name of the game when you two get together, as you don't always see eye to eye. After all, as a Taurean lass, you can dig your feet in when the mood suits you and stand your ground, come what may, and your Arien love gets impatient when folk don't immediately bend to his will, though he'd say they aren't seeing sense – his sense! Even so, he'll adore the way you always look your beautiful best, especially when you're out on the town together. What an adorable asset you are! The only thing you've got to watch is in the passion stakes – he can be fast and furious while you like to take things slowly, steadily and very sensuously indeed. Find the happy medium and it could be the start of something big!

TAURUS WOMAN AND TAURUS MAN

What a delightful duo you are! You've both got the same priorities in life, with creature comforts coming high on the list. There's nothing you like better than curling up at home in front of a big log fire, or sinking deep into enormous armchairs and thinking 'This is the life'! As a tender Taurean miss, you love looking after your other half, and if he's a boy Bull then he'll revel in every luxurious and hedonistic minute! What's more, you're both tremendously tactile and supremely sensual, so you believe in having lots of bear (or bull!) hugs and cosy cuddles whenever you get the chance. Emotionally you'll be in seventh heaven together, knowing that each of you believes in fidelity. In fact, you could be such a constant couple that you might decide to stay together even if your relationship's over in all but name – you just can't let go. Talk about tenacious Taurus!

TAURUS WOMAN AND GEMINI MAN

Life will be lovely when you two first start hitting the high spots together, but the burning question is will it last? You'll fall hook, line and sinker for your Mercurial man's captivating charm and ability to jolly you out of moods, and you'll be thrilled by the way he always seems to bump into a pal or acquaintance wherever you go. In return, he'll love you for taking things in your stride and adding an air of elegance and sophistication to every event. The trouble could come after a while when your Gemini lad wants to take off by himself leaving you at home. He'll tell you that he needs to live a life of his own, whereas you need your life to be shared between the two of you. Sexually, you could have a few hurdles to jump too, as you like making love with your hands, while your Gemini man uses his mind and imagination. Something's got to give, but what will it be?

TAURUS WOMAN AND CANCER MAN

Cherishing is the only way to describe your loving liaison, as you two are delighted to devote your lives to each other in a way that makes less lucky folk go green with envy. What's more, you both value emotional and physical security, so you'll want your abode to be your refuge from the stresses and strains of the outside world. Let's face it, you're both terrific homemakers! There's no need for you to wonder how the other one feels, as you're both so tactile, emotional and demonstrative that there may be no need for words. As a Taurean you're often plagued by possessive feelings and jealous outbursts, but there'll be no need for that with your Crabby chap as you'll try to be together for as many hours a day as possible, and you'd rather attend social soirées together than go on your ownsome. There's no doubt about it, when you fall for a Cancerian man the two of you could live happily ever after.

TAURUS WOMAN AND LEO MAN

Loyalty? It goes without saying when you two start stepping out together, as you're both fundamentally faithful and true. The problems start when that fidelity spills over into other areas of your affair, making you both determined, dogmatic and even dictatorial. You don't welcome any sort of change in your world, and your Leo lad believes that he's right – always! It can be hopeless if you try to have a discussion or debate, because it usually ends in stalemate, with both of you too proud or pedantic to back down one inch. Once you can learn to compromise, you'll be well on the way to a wonderful relationship in which you can pamper and pander to each other's needs and desires. He'll adore the way you always look a treat, and you'll look after him as only a Bullette can. Smashing!

TAURUS WOMAN AND VIRGO MAN

There's so much you can learn when you pal up with a Virgo chap, as he'll open your mind to all sorts of facts and figures, and his perceptive powers could help you over whatever hassles and hurdles life places in your path. You'll be fascinated, enthralled and delighted to have someone to depend on. There's just one problem – you need lots of love and affection from your amour; but can your Virgo chap fit the bill? You may be the apple of his eye but it'll give you the pip when he seems too busy paying bills or sorting out problems to give you more than just a peck on your rosy cheek.

You may have your sexual differences too, as you like your love to include lots of kisses and cuddles, and he may be a wee bit too distant or detached for that. You'll just have to use your powers of passionate persuasion!

TAURUS WOMAN AND LIBRA MAN

It's almost too good to be true when a Bullette meets a Libran lad! Suddenly you're surrounded by soft lights and sweet music which wafts over you courtesy of pretty Venus, your joint ruler. It's as though you were meant for each other, because your Libran amour has spent his life searching for the perfect and permanent partner, and you've always wanted to pair up with someone forever and a day. Sounds as though you're going to live happily ever after! There's just one word of warning – if your Venusian fella is one of those Libran libertines who has to try out his charms on every woman he meets, your jealous streak could soon get the better of you and lead to tears, tirades and tantrums. Even if he's only having a flirt, not a philander, you still won't like what you see.

TAURUS WOMAN AND SCORPIO MAN

Phew! Who turned the heating up? There's a torrid, florid and fervent feeling to your loving liaison that makes you irresistible to each other – talk about a fatal attraction! Once you've paired up you both believe that it's for life, and nothing will change that. In fact, even if it would be better to part and be happy, you'd rather stick together and stay miserable – somehow it seems more secure that way! You adore being together, but you've both got to cultivate outside hobbies, pals and pastimes if you want to keep your amour alive. One thing you won't take kindly to is the slightest suspicion that your Scorpio swain isn't being true to you – even the neighbours will know your feelings, 'cos you'll broadcast them loud and clear!

TAURUS WOMAN AND SAGITTARIUS MAN

East is east and west is west and never the twain shall meet. That could be the story of your lives together, 'cos you're poles apart. Unless you want this to be a very short-lived affair indeed you've got to find some middle ground that brings you together instead of driving you further apart. Your need for stability and security is utterly at odds with your Saggy man's love for challenge and adventure, which means you can find it almost impossible to understand each other's motives. It could cause all sorts of restrictions, rifts and ructions between you unless you can find some common interest quick. Cultural concerns could be just the ticket, as you'll be able to expand your artistic abilities together. You've also got to let your Archer go off by himself sometimes (without asking him where he's been when he returns!) or he may waltz out of the door one day and never come back.

TAURUS WOMAN AND CAPRICORN MAN

You're the tops! Whether it's business or pleasure, you two go together like champagne and caviare – or bread and water if you're feeling broke! As you're both Earth signs you understand what makes each other tick, and you need the material possessions that your Capricorn man can give you once he's achieved his ambition of reaching the top of the tree. Along the way you'll dole out help and encouragement to each other, and if you formed a business double act you'd soon be laughing all the way to the bank! Money plays a large part in your partnership, even if it's under the surface, as loot is something you both need. Another thing that you need is emotional security, and this Goaty guy can give you oodles of it! He may not deluge you with hearts and flowers, but he's got some very sensual and sentimental ways of showing that he cares. Be patient, and you'll see what I mean!

TAURUS WOMAN AND AQUARIUS MAN

What a dogmatic duo you are! You're both as stubborn as mules and immovable as mountains, which can spell disaster when the two of you get together. It's very difficult indeed for you to sort out any disagreements or dilemmas because neither of you can see any viewpoint but your own! One area where you can really clash and come to grief is in amour, 'cos you've got very different expectations indeed. As an emotional Bullette, you need lots of love and affection from your other half, plus a sensuous and sultry sex life, but that could be the last thing your Aquarian Adonis has got in mind. For a start, he'll find your possessive and jealous ways very hard to handle, and whenever he swans off into the sunset to do his own thing you won't like it one bit! He may also find it difficult to show his feelings, and you could both discover that this is a partnership full of problems.

39

TAURUS WOMAN AND PISCES MAN

Once you two meet you'll wonder how you ever survived apart! Even if you stay as friends and don't progress to passionate partners, you'll appreciate each other's finer qualities and refined, sophisticated and chic ways. Creative concerns of all kinds will fascinate and enthral you, and you'll love being seen in all the best places. There's no need for tears or sulky silences whenever an anniversary comes round because you're both such born romantics that you'll have etched the date in your diaries weeks before! What's more, you'll celebrate in style while bluebirds of happiness fly around you. The only problem that could blight your bliss will be if your Fishy fella decides to indulge his fancy for fantasy with other fanciable folk. Whether it's all in his imagination or hard fact, you'll view it as betrayal, which could provoke some very possessive and sticky scenes, or even spell the end of your affair.

MERCURY AND YOU

Ever had days when nothing's gone right? You know the sort – when you've missed meetings, transport's let you down, you've been at cross-purposes with a pal, or found that your phone's gone on the blink just when you need it most? Well, if it's any consolation, mischievous mini Mercury may have been the cause of all your problems.

You see, in astrology, this tiny planet rules all our communications, day-to-day dealings, everyday routines and short journeys, and he usually whizzes round the starry skies, hot on the heels of the super Sun (they're never more than 28° apart). However, every now and then he slows down in his tracks and appears to travel backwards – what astrologers call 'turning retrograde'. Whenever he does that, you need to be extra-careful about all your dealings with others, because that's when things can go wrong, with mishaps, misunderstandings and mistakes all more than likely to arise. On the other hand, when Mercury's fast-forwarding through a sign that's compatible with yours (either one that's two signs away or one belonging to the same element, such as Fire), communications should go with a swing. When Mercury moves through a sign that's not compatible with yours (either the Sun sign directly opposite yours or one of the same quality, such as Cardinal), things could be a wee bit troublesome, with discord, disharmony or disagreements in the air.

MERCURY AND YOU

Feeling worried? Well, don't be, for all you need to do is remember the motto 'Forewarned is forearmed', plot the progress of mini Mercury through the signs over the coming year, read the relevant paragraph and act accordingly. You'll find the tricky times much easier to cope with, and could go from strength to strength when Mercury's on your side!

SIGN	SYMBOL	RULER	ELEMENT	QUALITY
Aries	Ram	Mars	Fire	Cardinal
Taurus	Bull	Venus	Earth	Fixed
Gemini	Twins	Mercury	Air	Mutable
Cancer	Crab	Moon	Water	Cardinal
Leo	Lion	Sun	Fire	Fixed
Virgo	Virgin	Mercury	Earth	Mutable
Libra	Balance	Venus	Air	Cardinal
Scorpio	Scorpion	Mars Pluto	Water	Fixed
Sagittarius	Archer	Jupiter	Fire	Mutable
Capricorn	Goat	Saturn	Earth	Cardinal
Aquarius	Water Carrier	Saturn Uranus	Air	Fixed
Pisces	Fish	Jupiter Neptune	Water	Mutable

MERCURY'S ENTRY INTO THE SIGNS IN 1992

from 1 January	Sagittarius
10 January	Capricorn
29 January	Aquarius
16 February	Pisces
3 March	Aries
17 March	turns retrograde in Aries
4 April	Pisces
9 April	turns direct in Pisces
14 April	Aries
11 May	Taurus
26 May	Gemini
9 June	Cancer
27 June	Leo
20 July	turns retrograde in Leo
13 August	turns direct in Leo
3 September	Virgo
19 September	Libra
7 October	Scorpio
29 October	Sagittarius
11 November	turns retrograde in Sagittarius
21 November	Scorpio
2 December	turns direct in Scorpio
12 December	Sagittarius

MERCURY'S PROGRESS THROUGH THE ZODIAC

It's easy to plot Mercury's progress through the zodiac with the help of my chart on the next page, but there's even more you can learn about his effects on you through the coming months. When Mercury is in your Sun sign, he will occupy your first house, then when he moves into the next sign he'll be in your second house, and so on, until he eventually reaches your first house once more.

Whenever he changes signs and houses, Mercury affects a different aspect of your life, as you'll see as you read on. Using the picture of the zodiac wheel over the page, write in the number 1 by your Sun sign and continue in an anti-clockwise direction around the signs until you've completed them all. Then it will be easy for you to refer to this chart as you trace Mercury's movements in 1992. Good luck!

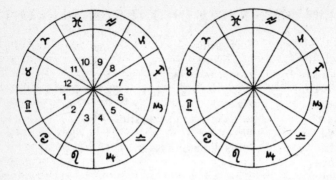

Astrological houses numbered for someone born with the Sun in Gemini.

Fill in this diagram and you'll be able to plot the course of Mercury through each of your astrological houses. Simply write the number 1 by your Sun sign and continue in an anti-clockwise direction around the zodiac wheel until you have completed all twelve.

MERCURY IN THE FIRST HOUSE

Ace! That's the only way to describe your daily doings, discourses and dealings with others now, for you're flying as high as a kite in all communicative concerns. With your mind as sharp as a razor and your brain buzzing with ideas, images, intelligence and inspiration, you'll burst if you don't express yourself and air your views at every available opportunity! Just make sure you don't hog the limelight, control every conversation or dominate every discussion, for otherwise folk will soon stop listening to you! Even so, this is the time to put new projects and plans into action, especially if that involves taking the initiative, talking things through or committing your ideas to paper. In fact, keeping track of your thoughts is a good idea now, because with your mind jumping from one thought to another like a brilliant butterfly, you could easily forget or overlook something important.

Negotiations and discussions will go well too, so start talking! Get out and about if you start to feel restless – you'll certainly enjoy yourself and you could even have an interesting experience or two along the way!

When Mercury turns retrograde in this house, you should pay extra attention to all personal concerns. Things may not go according to plan, you could make a silly slip-up or you might feel so restless you can't settle down to doing anything concrete at all. Go carefully!

MERCURY IN THE SECOND HOUSE

People, places, possessions, pursuits, persuasions or principles . . . Whatever you value in life will rarely be far from your thoughts now, making you cogitate, consider and contemplate whatever it is that makes your world go round. Maybe you'll get involved in a deep discussion about the things you hold most dear, or discover a new interest that's full of meaning for you?

Business matters and commercial ventures could also play an important part in your life now, making it a terrific time to state your terms, do some wheeling and dealing, or sell your talents to the highest bidder. Not only will folk be interested in what you've got to say, but you'll also be able to make precise plans and state your case clearly and concisely. You should have a good eye for a bargain if you're off on a shopping spree – and if you want to haggle over a price this is definitely the time to do it! Thinking of making a major purchase, such as a car or house? Then you'll find it easy to read and understand the small print before signing on the dotted line. It's also a grand opportunity to sort out your affluent affairs. Talk things over with money magnates, go through bank statements with a fine-tooth comb or sort out all your important papers so you know exactly where they are – and where you stand.

Money matters may be muddled and muddy when naughty Mercury moves backwards through the skies, so avoid buying anything big or committing yourself cashwise, and keep a close eye on current accounts, as computer slip-ups could cause chaos.

MERCURY IN THE THIRD HOUSE

Talk about having the gift of the gab! You'll hardly pause for breath as you chatter away about every subject under the Sun that interests you, and even a few that don't! Everyone, from close family and friends to folk you meet at the bus stop, will all be treated to your news and views, and enjoy a good old chinwag with you. What's more, if there's any gossip around, you're sure to be in the know! Intellectually, you're on top form – witty, eloquent and erudite – so don't let the grass grow under your feet whilst you're being so clever and capable. Instead, put pen to paper, get on the phone, air your ideas in discussions and debates, read an improving book or brush up your brainpower in any way that takes your fancy. Puzzles, quizzes and crosswords will be grist to your mill too – they won't tease your big brain for long!

Feeling rather restless? You'll find it hard to relax by sitting still and taking life easy now, because you're just not in the mood, so give yourself a break instead by heading off on a short journey, day trip or jolly junket with a few friends. Who knows who you might meet along the way?

Communications could be chaotic if Mercury retraces his steps whilst in this house. Letters may go on the missing list, phone messages might never be returned, or you could get completely the wrong end of the stick over something simple or silly. It's not a time to take chances with any important missives or money matters, especially if you're about to clinch a deal or agreement. Instead, try to hold fire until mini Mercury's back on course, when you can forge full steam ahead once more.

MERCURY IN THE FOURTH HOUSE

Put on your thinking cap! You've had such a busy time over the past couple of months that you need to retreat into your shell and mull over at your leisure all your recent ideas, experiences and encounters. Whilst you're about it, put family matters and domestic details on the agenda too, and have a good hard think about whether or not your home life offers you everything you need. Keeping quiet or acting the martyr, instead of saying what you think, will only make matters worse, as you'll soon start to feel resentful – so speak your mind and let your nearest and dearest do the same. There's a lot you could learn as a result! Want to give the old homestead a face-lift? Then start making plans pronto, but don't forget to ask the rest of the family for their ideas as well!

Nostalgic thoughts are never far away now, so have a lovely meander down Memory Lane, look through your mementoes or talk over old times with someone special. Visiting your family, organising a gathering of the clans, or having a heart-to-heart with a dear one will also provide you with plenty of food for thought.

Thinking about a past event might even solve a present problem, or reveal the reason for a person's perverse or bad behaviour, so get those memories going.

Keep a close eye on domestic dealings when Mercury starts to back-pedal on his planetary path, especially if you're moving house or altering your abode in some way, for mistakes may easily be made. You could find you're at cross-purposes with a relative, too, so make sure there's no room for misunderstandings.

MERCURY IN THE FIFTH HOUSE

Got something to say? Then now's the time to speak up and broadcast your thoughts to the waiting world! All sorts of fun, frivolous or fantastic ideas, as well as some captivating creative concepts, could be flooding your mind. Don't dismiss them out of hand, for one could be a sure-fire winner. Burying your bonce in a good book or putting your thoughts on paper will be enjoyable, especially if you can use your little grey cells and give your brain some exercise. You might even pick up some fascinating facts or important information along the way!

You'll love being with wee kids or light-hearted adults right now, for you're all on the same wavelength and will enjoy each other's company. Watch out, though, if you fancy playing a prank or practical joke on someone – what seems hilarious to you could be horrendous to them, so think twice before swinging into action! Another possible problem may arise if you're so wrapped up in your own ideas, opinions and occupations that you seem supremely selfish, ignoring the needs of your nearest and dearest or chiming into every conversation until no one else can get a word in edgeways! Try to give others a chance to speak sometimes!

Dealings with dear ones could be covered in confusion when Mercury turns retrograde, so be prepared! Maybe an eagerly awaited love letter goes astray, a silly spat separates you from a sweetheart or a child plays you up in no uncertain terms. Someone could also be speaking with a forked tongue, so don't believe everything you hear!

MERCURY IN THE SIXTH HOUSE

Meticulous, methodical and matter of fact – that's the only way to describe you at the moment, thanks to your practical, pragmatic, precise and perfectionist persona. Whatever you tackle will be done to the very best of your ability, and even if you usually rush through things, you won't be taking short cuts or cutting any corners now. What an asset you are! Bosses, colleagues and clients will all be delighted to have you around, especially if there are problems to be solved or piles of paperwork to be pored over. Meetings, discussions or pow-wows will also show you at your best, for you'll be able to put your ideas forward without blowing your own trumpet or appearing to make yourself the centre of attention. It's also a fine time to get any working hassles or hitches out into the open and to talk them through with the folk concerned. Want to find a new job? Then get on the phone or start writing letters now, whilst you're such a good advertisement for your own talents!

Health, hygiene and other medical matters could interest you now, whether you're embarking on a new diet or exercise regime, or just want to find out more about keeping fit. Watch out if you start to feel cross or critical, for you could easily let your tongue run away with you and trample over friends' finer feelings without even realising it. Think before you speak!

Workaday dealings may well hit setbacks or snags when Mercury moves backwards through this house, and making appointments with doctors or dentists may be well-nigh impossible for one reason or another. Your nerves might also make you feel jumpy, jangled and jazzed-up, so try to relax. Come on, take a deep breath!

MERCURY IN THE SEVENTH HOUSE

Two heads are better than one! That's the message to remember now if you want to make the most of the coming weeks, so pair up with like-minded folk at every opportunity! Getting a plan or project off the launching pad will be much more successful if you're part of a team, so pal up pronto! It's also a good idea to share your views, opinions and thoughts with folk on the same wavelength. Even if you just have a nice natter over a noggin, it'll help you to clarify your own ideas, and you'll also learn some interesting facts and figures along the way. So don't go it alone now, for you'll miss out on a whole host of opportunities, openings and outlooks!

If your one-to-one affairs have been tricky, troublesome or tense lately, then this is your chance to get problems out in the open at long last. Discuss your difficulties with the folk concerned and clear the air – you'll be glad you made the effort.

Stimulating company, intellectual companions or mentally-motivated mates will all bring out the best in you now, so mix and mingle with folk who've got something interesting to say, or get chatting to your other half about some serious-minded subjects or controversial concerns.

Partnerships could prove problematic while Mercury's retracing his steps through this house. Rows may arise over nothing at all, mistakes might abound or an appointment to meet a pal could go awry when both of you set out for different rendezvous. Try to avoid important negotiations or contracts that need signing until Mercury's back on course – better safe than sorry!

MERCURY IN THE EIGHTH HOUSE

Still waters will run deep over the next few weeks, when your thoughts take a very profound, probing and perceptive turn indeed. Chats and chinwags with your other half could cover some stupendously serious subjects, as you discuss all sorts of meaningful matters, intimate affairs or important aspects of everyday life. You may develop a new understanding of what makes you both tick, so don't be afraid to speak your mind. You might also meet someone who seems to know exactly what you're thinking, or agrees with everything you say, making all your conversations seem like quite uncanny experiences. Kismet?

Got a problem or question about your mortgage, pension, insurance, tax affairs, VAT or other official money matters? Then sort things out fast by talking or writing to informative financial folk who'll put you in the picture. This is also a good opportunity to go through all your papers, throwing away anything that's out of date and making sure you've got all the right forms and documents, especially if they're concerned with shared affairs or joint accounts.

You'll need to be on your toes whenever Mercury goes into reverse in this solar sphere, for that's when any affluent affairs you share with others could come in for a clobbering. Keep a close eye on joint accounts, as one of you may drain the boodle bag dry – or perhaps a silly slip-up over the pounds and pence causes no end of trouble? Make sure your eyes are peeled in all pecuniary or passionate pursuits!

MERCURY IN THE NINTH HOUSE

Fresh fields and pastures new! They're what you're hankering for right now, so grab any chance to expand your world and broaden the boundaries of your brain, even if only from the depths of your armchair! You're eager to learn more about the world you live in, so do some serious reading, watch a mind-stretching TV programme or discuss your views with your most brainy and brilliant buddies. Joining an environmental or ecological group could also appeal, especially if it involves getting out and about and meeting lots of fascinating folk.

Want to give your brain cells a good airing? Then how about enrolling in an evening class or correspondence course in order to discover more about a subject that's always intrigued you? There's more than a hint of cosmopolitan concerns in the air, so it's a grand time to learn a new language or discover more about another creed, culture or country. If you've got the chance to go one better and jet off to a faraway place on holiday, then you couldn't have picked a better time! Visiting somewhere steeped in history will be well worth while, especially if the way of life there is nothing like your own. You're really keen on seeing how the other half lives right now!

Travel won't be all plain sailing when Mercury's taking a return journey through the heavens, so don't trust to luck or take any chances. You could leave the tickets or your passport behind, miss the plane by minutes or find your train timetable's out of date. Better be on your guard at all times!

MERCURY IN THE TENTH HOUSE

Best foot forward! This isn't the time to rest on your laurels, for the more you use your brain, the more rewards and achievements will await you. Ever wished you had more qualifications, or are you longing to learn a new skill? Then get cracking now by enquiring about courses or classes, and you'll soon be able to add another string to your many-talented bow.

If that doesn't appeal, then have a think about the direction your life is taking. Are you happy with the way things are, or do you feel you've missed the boat or let someone else grab all the glory that's rightfully yours? If so, then maybe it's time to switch tactics, make important changes or cut your losses. This is also a smashing chance to talk to bosses, bureaucrats and bigwigs about any professional or prestigious problems and pitfalls that may be plaguing you, for you'll be able to state your case concisely and be sure of a receptive response. Clear the air and iron out any misunderstandings or muddles with parents, older folk or father figures whilst you're about it, and you'll be relieved and relaxed as a result. Isn't that better?

Filling in forms or sorting out red tape will be easier than usual now, but beware of getting so caught up in petty procedures and trifling topics that you can't see the wood for the trees!

Don't commit yourself to any agreements that are irrevocable or unbreakable whilst Mercury's in retreat, or you could find that you're saddled with a pig in a poke, or haven't been given all the facts. Professional paperwork, office memos or official documents might go missing too, so keep track of anything important!

MERCURY IN THE ELEVENTH HOUSE

Are you well on the way to achieving your aims and ambitions, or have you a sneaking suspicion that you're on a losing wicket? Well, this is your chance to put all your hopes, dreams and schemes under the mental microscope, and work out whether they're rooted in reality or are just plain pie in the sky. If they're more fiction than fact, then this is when you can get them back on course, making whatever changes or concessions are necessary.

Pastimes or hobbies that tax your brain and set you thinking are starred for success now, especially if they bring you in touch with like-minded folk or push you out into the wide, wide world. Getting together with friends and acquaintances will also be extra-enjoyable, especially if you can indulge in some dazzling discussions, clever conversations or educated exchanges. One thing's for sure – you've no patience with dolts, dullards or ditherers now, so surround yourself instead with folk who'll make good sparring partners for your rapier-like mind.

Been feeling lonely lately? Then how about joining a new club, group or society, especially if it's got an intellectual or humanitarian slant? Not only will you get to know lots of fascinating folk, but you'll also gain a fresh outlook on life – what more could you wish for?

Watch out if Mercury does a U-turn in this house, for you may meet someone who's determined to impose their prejudices, preconceptions and preconceived ideas on you. Listen to what they've got to say, and then make up your mind!

MERCURY IN THE TWELFTH HOUSE

Talk about being in a brown study! Rather than throw yourself into the social swing at the moment, you'd rather retreat far from the madding crowd to contemplate, cogitate and concentrate in peace. Perhaps there's a particular problem you want to mull over at your leisure, or maybe you just aren't in the mood for being around others? Either way, a spot of deep thinking by yourself will do you the world of good and help to put matters into their proper perspective. As well as wondering about other folk's actions, spare some time to brood over your own behaviour – especially if that involves delving into the darker and deeper corners of your character. There's a lot you could learn about yourself now, so don't be afraid to face up to your faults or acknowledge your fears and phobias. Because you're in such a meditative mood, working by yourself will make you happiest, and it's a grand time to do some research or serious study, too.

All the same, don't spend so much time by yourself that you fall into a deep depression or avoid dealing with difficulties that need urgent attention. If conversations or discussions take a tricky turn, you may prefer to keep mum rather than say what you think, in case your plain talk puts someone's back up. However, staying silent could cause even more conflict, so speak up and get your feelings off your chest. Remember, honesty is your best policy now.

Beware of skeletons tumbling out of cupboards or secrets seeing the light of day when Mercury backtracks through this solar abode. Being gullible or naive could also land you in trouble, as folk may not be as straightforward as they seem. Watch out!

DISCOVER AND DEVELOP
YOUR HIDDEN POTENTIAL
WITH GENEROUS JUPITER

Ever had the nagging feeling that you're not making the most of your abilities, or want to switch jobs or professions but don't know what to plump for next? Then you can let wise old Jupiter point you in the right direction by discovering his position at the time of your birth. Astrologers take the whole of someone's birth chart into consideration before reaching any conclusions about his or her character, but even so, this brief guide to Jupiter's planetary positions will give you a good idea of where your true potential lies, so that you can make the most of the opportunities that come your way. All you need do is check down the list to find which sign Jupiter occupied when you were born, then read the section on that particular placing to learn all about your abilities, talents and positive points. It could be the start of a whole new way of life!

Ginormous Jupiter is the largest planet in our solar system, so it's hardly surprising that he rules expansion – both physical and mental. As you will see from the list of Jupiter's movements this century, his orbit can be quite erratic as he moves back and forth between some signs and sweeps straight through others. On the whole, though, it takes him twelve years to complete one cycle through the zodiac.

DISCOVER YOUR POTENTIAL WITH JUPITER

Jupiter has a very strong influence on our outlook on life, and is associated with optimism, good luck, opportunities, success and happiness, as well as religion, politics, philosophy, history and the search for knowledge. If Jupiter is strongly placed in your birth chart, you can be an entrepreneur, have a very positive approach to life, and be jovial, loyal, benevolent and blessed with good intellectual powers. On the other hand, if Jupiter is badly placed or receives lots of tense aspects from other planets (only an astrologer will be able to tell you this), you could be overly optimistic, never know when to say no, have extremist beliefs, be conceited and even self-indulgent.

Every twelve years, genial Jupiter returns to the precise position he occupied at the time of your birth (astrologers call this a Jupiter Return), heralding a time when your income could increase, opportunities and openings may come your way and life takes on a very rosy hue indeed. Check the chart to see when jolly Jupiter last revisited his natal position, then add twelve years on from that to discover when his next visit will be, and then prepare to make the most of what promises to be a positive, propitious and prosperous period! Perfect!

JUPITER'S MOVEMENTS THROUGH THE YEARS

1 January 1910	Libra
11 November 1910	Scorpio
10 December 1911	Sagittarius
5 January 1913	Capricorn
21 January 1914	Aquarius
4 February 1915	Pisces
12 February 1916	Aries
26 June 1916	Taurus
27 October 1916	Aries
13 February 1917	Taurus
30 June 1917	Gemini
13 July 1918	Cancer
2 August 1919	Leo
27 August 1920	Virgo
26 September 1921	Libra
27 October 1922	Scorpio
25 November 1923	Sagittarius
18 December 1924	Capricorn
6 January 1926	Aquarius
18 January 1927	Pisces
6 June 1927	Aries
11 September 1927	Pisces
23 January 1928	Aries
4 June 1928	Taurus
13 June 1929	Gemini
27 June 1930	Cancer
17 July 1931	Leo
11 August 1932	Virgo
10 September 1933	Libra
11 October 1934	Scorpio
9 November 1935	Sagittarius
2 December 1936	Capricorn
20 December 1937	Aquarius
14 May 1938	Pisces
30 July 1938	Aquarius
30 December 1938	Pisces
12 May 1939	Aries
30 October 1939	Taurus
21 December 1939	Aries

16 May 1940	Taurus
27 May 1941	Gemini
10 June 1942	Cancer
1 July 1943	Leo
26 July 1944	Virgo
25 August 1945	Libra
25 September 1946	Scorpio
24 October 1947	Sagittarius
15 November 1948	Capricorn
13 April 1949	Aquarius
28 June 1949	Capricorn
1 December 1949	Aquarius
15 April 1950	Pisces
15 September 1950	Aquarius
2 December 1950	Pisces
22 April 1951	Aries
29 April 1952	Taurus
10 May 1953	Gemini
24 May 1954	Cancer
13 June 1955	Leo
17 November 1955	Virgo
18 January 1956	Leo
8 July 1956	Virgo
13 December 1956	Libra
20 February 1957	Virgo
7 August 1957	Libra
14 January 1958	Scorpio
21 March 1958	Libra
7 September 1958	Scorpio
11 February 1959	Sagittarius
25 April 1959	Scorpio
6 October 1959	Sagittarius
2 March 1960	Capricorn
10 June 1960	Sagittarius
26 October 1960	Capricorn
15 March 1961	Aquarius
12 August 1961	Capricorn
11 November 1961	Aquarius
26 March 1962	Pisces
4 April 1963	Aries

12 April 1964	Taurus
23 April 1965	Gemini
21 September 1965	Cancer
17 November 1965	Gemini
6 May 1966	Cancer
28 September 1966	Leo
16 January 1967	Cancer
23 May 1967	Leo
19 October 1967	Virgo
27 February 1968	Leo
16 June 1968	Virgo
16 November 1968	Libra
31 March 1969	Virgo
16 July 1969	Libra
17 December 1969	Scorpio
30 April 1970	Libra
16 August 1970	Scorpio
14 January 1971	Sagittarius
5 June 1971	Scorpio
12 September 1971	Sagittarius
7 February 1972	Capricorn
25 July 1972	Sagittarius
26 September 1972	Capricorn
23 February 1973	Aquarius
8 March 1974	Pisces
18 March 1975	Aries
26 March 1976	Taurus
23 August 1976	Gemini
17 October 1976	Taurus
4 April 1977	Gemini
20 August 1977	Cancer
1 January 1978	Gemini
12 April 1978	Cancer
5 September 1978	Leo
1 March 1979	Cancer
20 April 1979	Leo
29 September 1979	Virgo
27 October 1980	Libra
30 November 1981	Scorpio
31 December 1982	Sagittarius

25 January 1984	Capricorn
7 February 1985	Aquarius
20 February 1986	Pisces
2 March 1987	Aries
8 March 1988	Taurus
22 July 1988	Gemini
30 November 1988	Taurus
11 March 1989	Gemini
31 July 1989	Cancer
18 August 1990	Leo
12 September 1991	Virgo
10 October 1992	Libra

JUPITER IN ARIES

Terrific! It's second nature for you to make the most of your attributes and talents – and to bring them to the attention of every-one around you! You find it easy to blow your own trumpet, but just make sure you don't do it too often or too loudly, or you'll put people off! (This won't be a possible problem if you've got the Sun in Virgo, because your innate modesty will exert a restraining influence.)

One thing's for sure – you're broad-minded, enthusiastic, optimistic, adventurous and assertive. You're also imbued with plenty of the pioneering spirit – holidays spent exploring new lands, going on safari or taking some dare-devil risks are all ideal for you! Any occupations that make the most of your enterprising and competitive character should do well, and you may well be super at sports. In fact, anything safe, stolid or sedentary makes you see red (when you drive it's often in a very fast and furious fashion!), so try to inject as much excitement into your life as possible. Coping with small details may be difficult, but you're a wow when it comes to taking overall views or making grand plans. Think big!

JUPITER IN TAURUS

Food, glorious food! That's your theme tune, for there's no doubt you go gooey over gorgeous grub and grog. In fact, it's almost impossible for you to resist the sweet and succulent things of life, especially when you're feeling a wee bit blue. There's just one thing to remember – Jupiter rules expansion, and accumulating the avoir-dupois could be a real problem for you! Never mind, for your gorgeously generous nature and smashing sense of humour means you brim over with benevolence and bonhomie, making you a very popular person indeed. You love entertaining at home and watching others enjoy themselves, so any jobs that have you acting as a host or hostess will suit you down to the ground.

You're a marvel on the financial front as well, and have an uncanny knack for making little acorns of affluence grow into giant oaks of prosperity. Making the most of your brilliant business sense is another good idea, for your cautious character and commendable common sense will ensure steady pecuniary progress whilst ruling out any risk-taking. Sounds like you're on to a winner!

JUPITER IN GEMINI

Brilliant, brainy and broad-minded, that's you! Your intellect and intelligence are second to none, but channelling those marvellous mental methods into successful schemes and completed projects can be very difficult indeed. The trouble is you're spoilt for choice. Your enquiring and curious mind is always discovering new interests and enthusiasms, so you flit from one to another without finishing what you've started. If it's well-nigh impossible for you to concentrate on a particular project for protracted periods, why not make the most of your versatility by opting for occupations where you never know what will happen next? Being stuck behind a desk will drive you to distraction, but jobs connected with travel, the media or buying and selling could be just what you need.

Because it's natural for you to look on the bright side, folk love having you around, and your ready wit, cheery chat and verbal gymnastics all place you high in the popularity polls. Your gift of the gab also means you can talk your way out of the trickiest situations, which is just as well, for you often land yourself in them!

JUPITER IN CANCER

Caring, considerate, charitable, compassionate, cherishing . . . You've got a heart as big as a house! Anyone coming to you for sympathy or TLC (tender loving care) can be sure of a warm welcome, lots of love and some sensible advice. In fact, you're often the one folk turn to when they need a shoulder to cry on, thanks to your ability to empathise with them and tune into their inner thoughts and needs. You can't walk past people collecting for charity without putting some pennies in their tins either! Not surprisingly, any profession or vocation that brings out these sterling qualities will fill you with satisfaction, and even a part-time project that helps others (especially children or old folk) will do the trick.

You probably love collecting little knick-knacks and other items of interest, and your brilliant business sense means you've got an eye for a bargain and can snap up things in junk shops that turn out to be real antiques! Ever thought of doing it for a living? Cooking is another of your strong points, and although you adore conjuring up vast vats of fabulous food for your nearest and dearest, it's also a possible profession. Making the most of your marvellous memory and vivid imagination will also bring home the bacon. What a wonder you are!

JUPITER IN LEO

Talk about making a splash! You're usually so full of *joie de vivre* that it's almost impossible not to notice you, thanks to your exciting, extrovert and extravagant ways. Taking centre stage and basking in the limelight is of prime importance to you (you're a born star!), but sometimes that goes to your head, making you a wee bit of a show-off, or even rather pompous and puffed up with your own importance. Why not let your colossal creativity speak for itself rather than brag about all your talents? Anything associated with the stage or painting should bring out the best in you, and teaching young kids might also appeal.

Thinking big is your watchword, and you never do things by halves or settle for second best. You need to make lots of cash, because you love spending it, but your huge heart also means you're generous to a fault and lavish lots of luxuries on loved ones. Looking for some new clothes? Then you'll buy the best you can afford, especially if you know you'll cut a dramatic dash as a result! Organising others comes easily to you, and your love of life and infectious enthusiasm make you an excellent leader. Well, let's face it, you hate being told what to do! There's no doubt you're packed with potential, so come on, make the most of it!

JUPITER IN VIRGO

You're no fool! In fact, you're careful, cautious and critical to a discriminating degree, and usually look before you leap. You only accept a challenge when you've examined all the angles and aspects and know exactly where you stand, and your judgement is often spot-on. Trouble is, all that common sense can hold you back from taking risks or doing things on the spur of the moment, even when you'd like to. Never mind, for your matter-of-fact, methodical and sensible approach to life stands you in smashing stead and makes you a very valuable person to have around. Your self-confidence can be sadly lacking and hold you back at times, but thinking positive and reflecting on past glories will help you to bounce back.

You're much better at dealing with details than adopting an overall approach, and you'd make a terrific teacher. You may also be a born writer, for you can put your feelings into words, and are blessed with the concentration and dedication to keep you going through the bad times as well as the good. Work involving machines could go well too, for you're full of scientific and technical talents, and you're precise and practical to boot. There's a lot more to you than meets the eye, isn't there?

JUPITER IN LIBRA

Love, laughter, leisure and luxury – they're what you want out of life! Your kind, charming, convivial and vivacious personality gives you plenty of pals, and you enjoy entertaining them at home or going out on the town together for a slap-up meal. Being with loved ones is also of prime importance to you, and you make sure they know just how much you care. In fact, you're really at your best in a partnership, whether it's platonic, passionate or professional. You're a valuable part of any team, for your dislike of discord or disagreement means you'll always try to keep things happy and harmonious. You're also grand at encouraging others and infecting them with your own enthusiasm, so don't go it alone when you can pair up with like-minded folk instead – you'll find it much more worthwhile.

Your love of the finer things of life could also stand you in good stead when it comes to jobs, and anything associated with decorating, furnishings or *objets d'art* could be right up your street. Trouble is, you'd much rather watch others getting on with some hard work than do it yourself, so tackling tedious or tiresome tasks can be well-nigh impossible! Even so, you're packed with potential, so find things you really enjoy doing and then off you go!

JUPITER IN SCORPIO

Strong stuff! You're imbued with determination, willpower and considerable get-up-and-go, making you quite a formidable force to be reckoned with. In fact, you throw yourself wholeheartedly into everything you tackle, because you aren't happy unless you can feel emotionally involved in everything you do. Some folk go through life in a half-hearted manner but you're the exact opposite, and your problems often stem from doing too much rather than too little. Moderation? You don't know the meaning of the word! What you must beware of is wearing yourself out, either physically or emotionally, for you just don't know when to stop!

Your generosity often knows no bounds, but even so, you won't land yourself in a pecuniary pickle, for you're adept at affluent affairs and may even be a bit of a financial whizz kid on the quiet, especially when it comes to investing your hard-earned loot. Because of your profound powers of concentration, you're excellent at doing research or study (as long as it's on a topic that interests you), and criminological concerns could also prove intriguing. 'True grit' is another way to describe you, for you'll take even the most fraught or frightening facts in your stalwart and stoic stride. You're a great person to have around in a crisis!

JUPITER IN SAGITTARIUS

Congratulations! With generous Jupiter occupying his own sign of sagacious Sagittarius, there's a lot you can gain from this positive placing. Intellectually you're ace, and the more time you spend learning more about what life has to offer, the happier you'll be. Although you're interested in many subjects, you're also able to explore them in depth, especially if they're connected with history, philosophy, religion or languages. Life will never be long enough for you to cram in all the things you want to do, and even when you're eighty you'll still have a list as long as your arm, of projects and plans you've yet to tackle! You never stop learning – and that, along with your overwhelming optimism, is what makes you such captivating company. In fact, if you're ever feeling depressed, stagnant and stale, it may well be because you're not using your brain to its best advantage. Grab a good book, quick!

Keeping off the weight could be a problem, especially in later years, so why not fight the flab with some exercise or sporty pursuits? Just watch out for that devil-may-care streak of yours, or you could come a cropper! Any activities associated with writing or publishing are ideal for you, and travelling could also fill you with satisfaction, especially if you're off to far-away places with strong historical or cultural connections. Bon voyage!

JUPITER IN CAPRICORN

Slow and steady wins the race! Your resourceful, responsible and reliable approach to life means that once you've got a goal in your sights, you'll gradually work towards it until you've achieved your aims and come up trumps. It's no use hoping for sudden jumps up the ladder of success, for you must climb it rung by rung. Your considerable powers of concentration are another asset, and help you complete any task you tackle. You've a strong sense of duty and obligation which attracts many admirers (bosses and VIPs are especially impressed by your commendable character), but sometimes this serious attitude to life can overwhelm you, plunging you into pessimism or dragging you down into a deep depression. In fact, that's a trait you may have to fight, especially if you've got the Sun in Capricorn as well. Family ties mean a lot to you, but they can also be constricting, so take care!

Even so, your superb sense of humour usually saves the day, making you laugh at yourself and entertaining everyone around you. You won't be happy unless your occupation or profession stimulates your mind and provides you with a constant challenge, and if it also carries responsibility, then so much the better! In fact, any activity that promises prominence, praise or prestige is just what you need to bring out the very best in you. Good luck!

JUPITER IN AQUARIUS

The strong streak of humanitarianism that runs through you influences all your thoughts, words and deeds, making you stand out from the crowd and earning you a horde of fans. You've also got a powerful sense of justice and fair play, and since you can't abide seeing folk being taken for a ride, deceived or duped, you often get involved in fighting their cause or helping them to stand up for themselves. Ever thought of doing that for a living, as a voluntary worker, or what about joining a society that defends the rights of others? You could find it's the ideal grist to your mill!

Speaking of social set-ups, friends mean a lot to you, and you've probably amassed masses of mates from all walks of life. Even so, your independent and original nature means you can't abide tagging along behind others or going along with the gang just for the sake of it. Instead, you'd much rather paddle your own canoe and forge full steam ahead in your own inimitable style. Let's face it, you could even elevate a few eyebrows as you express yourself in whichever way comes most naturally! What's more, some of your inventive, intellectual and inspired ideas and attitudes could be streets ahead of everyone else's, so don't discount them out of hand or let others talk you out of following your star. The sky's the limit!

JUPITER IN PISCES

Compassionate, caring and considerate – does that sound like you? You may be so modest that it doesn't, but you can be sure that friends and family think otherwise. The milk of human kindness cascades through your veins, making you eager to help anyone in need and ensuring that you're always ready with a sympathetic shoulder for others to cry on. You'd do well in any of the caring professions, and even working as a part-time counsellor or helper would fill you with a strong sense of satisfaction and do a lot of good at the same time. On the other hand, you may already have your hands full listening to the problems of pals, partners and the whole family circle! Just make sure you aren't bogged down by other folk's tales of woe. Working with animals is another good idea, for you're instinctively in tune with them, so supporting an animal charity or helping out at a rescue centre are both good ideas. If you own any pets yourself, I'll bet they're treated like royalty!

Make the most of your incredible imagination, intuition and emotion in whichever way suits you best, but don't smother these feelings or they could turn you into someone who worries and frets about anything and everything. Your beliefs, creeds and principles, whether they're religious, spiritual or philosophical, will go very deep indeed, and you always try to practise what you preach. You're a lesson to us all!

RUSSELL'S SUN SIGN TRAVEL GUIDE

SUN SIGNS	TOWNS AND CITIES	COUNTRIES
Aries	Birmingham, Brunswick, Florence, Krakow, Leicester, Marseilles, Utrecht, Verona	Argentina, Denmark, England, France, Germany, Iran, Poland, Syria, Zimbabwe
Taurus	Dublin, Eastbourne, Hastings, Leipzig, Lucerne, Mantua, Palermo, Parma, St Louis	Afghanistan, Austria, Capri, Cyprus, Greek Islands, Ireland, Ischia, Israel, Japan, Norway, Switzerland
Gemini	Bruges, Cardiff, Cordoba, London, Melbourne, Metz, New York, Nuremburg, Plymouth, San Francisco, Versailles	Armenia, Belgium, Denmark, Egypt, Jordan, Sardinia, South Africa, Wales
Cancer	Algiers, Amsterdam, Berne, Cadiz, Genoa, Istanbul, Manchester, Milan, Stockholm, Tunis, Venice, York	Algeria, Canada, Holland, New Zealand, North and West Africa, Paraguay, Scotland

Leo	Bath, Bristol, Bombay, Chicago, Damascus, Los Angeles, Madrid, Philadelphia, Portsmouth, Prague, Rome, Syracuse	Chad, Cyprus, Czechoslovakia, Italy, Jamaica, Lebanon, Romania, Sicily, Spain
Virgo	Athens, Boston, Corinth, Heidelberg, Jerusalem, Paris, Reading, most spas and health resorts	Belize, Brazil, Bulgaria, Crete, Lower Silesia, Turkey, West Indies, Yugoslavia
Libra	Antwerp, Copenhagen, Freiburg, Frankfurt, Leeds, Lisbon, Nottingham, Vienna	Alsace, Austria, Burma, China, France, Japan, New Zealand, Tibet
Scorpio	Baltimore, Cincinnati, Dover, Fez, Hull, Halifax, Liverpool, Milwaukee, Newcastle-upon-Tyne, New Orleans, Stockport, Washington DC	Bavaria, Korea, Morocco, Norway, Poland, the Transvaal, Uruguay, USSR
Sagittarius	Avignon, Bradford, Budapest, Cologne, Naples, Nottingham, Sheffield, Stuttgart, Toledo, Toronto	Arabia, Australia, Hungary, Kenya, Yugoslavia, Zaire
Capricorn	Brussels, Constanta, Delhi, Oxford, Mecklenburg, Mexico City, Port Said, the administrative or bureaucratic centres of capital cities	Afghanistan, Albania, Bulgaria, Cuba, Lithuania, Mexico, the Orkneys, Saudi Arabia, Saxony, the Shetland Isles, Sweden
Aquarius	Bremen, Hamburg, Moscow	Ethiopia, Hungary, India, Iran, Israel, Poland, Yugoslavia

| Pisces | Alexandria, Bournemouth, Compostella, Seville | Brazil, many small Mediterranean islands, Pakistan, Portugal, the Sahara, Scandinavia |

THE TRADITIONS OF ASTROLOGY

SIGN	NOs	COLOUR	DAY	STONE	METAL	FLOWER	BODY AREA
Aries	1	Red	Tuesday	Diamond	Iron	Geranium	Head
Taurus	2	Copper, dark blue	Friday	Emerald	Copper	Daisy	Throat
Gemini	3	Yellows	Wednesday	Agate, garnet	Mercury	Daffodil	Hands, chest
Cancer	4	Pearl, silver	Monday	Pearl	Silver	White rose, lily	Breast
Leo	5	Amber, gold	Sunday	Ruby	Gold	Sunflower	Heart, spine
Virgo	6	Autumnal shades	Wednesday	Peridot	Mercury	Lily of the valley	Intestines
Libra	7	Pastel blues and pinks	Friday	Sapphire	Copper	Rose	Kidneys
Scorpio	8	Black, burgundy	Tuesday	Opal	Iron	Dahlia, rhododendron	Sexual organs
Sagittarius	9	Imperial purple	Thursday	Topaz	Tin	Delphinium	Thighs, hips
Capricorn	10, 1	Black, grey, white	Saturday	Turquoise	Lead	Pansy	Shins, knees
Aquarius	11, 2	Turquoise, blues	Saturday	Amethyst	Lead	Crocus, snowdrop	Ankles
Pisces	12, 3	Greens, sea blues	Thursday	Aquamarine	Tin	Poppy	Feet

WHAT 1992 HAS IN STORE
FOR YOUR
LOVE, CASH AND WORK

LOVE

Super-duper! Bluebirds of happiness have got you surrounded in nectarine 1992, so get ready to lie back and enjoy yourself! All amorous affairs look luscious during the opening months of the year, when your fond feelings for someone could grow into some very expressive emotions indeed. If you're a single Bull, then throwing yourself into the social swing might soon change all that, when you meet an inamorata who's irresistible! A creative concern or artistic activity could also win your heart and give you a completely new reason for living, as well as develop all sorts of talents you never knew you had.

Setting off for a far-flung land or about to enrol in an educational or environmental course? Then don't be surprised if you meet someone who sweeps you off your feet, even if they do come from another country, clime or culture or have views that are chalk to your cheese. It's time to live a little!

For some of you, major changes and massive upheavals have been working their way through your one-to-one affairs, and I'm sorry to say you're not out of the woods yet. Maybe you're reluctant to realise that a relationship has reached the end of the road, or maybe you're turning a blind eye to your other half's misdemeanours? Whatever's wrong, pretending it isn't happening will only make matters worse, so face up to the facts and start sorting them out. Out of bad does come good, I promise.

CASH

Cashing in on your creativity is the key to success as the annum unfolds, so make the most of your talents and attributes in whichever way comes naturally. Writing, painting, cooking or anything else that takes your fancy will be rewarding and remunerative, so don't hide your light under a bushel! You could also strike it lucky in competitions, prizes and raffles, so try your hand at them – after all, someone's got to win! It's also a grand time for splashing out the pounds and pence on love, leisure and pleasure, but the danger is you could easily get carried away and spend far more than you meant to, even if you do enjoy yourself whilst it lasts! Better work out a budget and stick to it like glue if you're up a gum tree financially.

Once the autumn arrives the affluent accent alters to your working world. Putting your shoulder to the wheel will bring boodle your way now, especially if your daily dealings are connected with health, medicine or being of service to others. Make the most of your pragmatic and practical personality, and money may not be far behind.

If your professional or prestigious pursuits are starting to suffer from setbacks, snags or stalemates then don't be shocked if they strain the strings of your purse. Booking up for the holiday of a lifetime? Then be careful to read the small print, otherwise it could cost you more than you bargained for. Ouch!

WORK

There's no doubt that work comes high on your agenda over the next year, but it may not always be quite what you expect! A promotion or better job could well be in the offing, but extra responsibilities, obligations and duties could be part of the proferred package. If you've been working hard over the past few years and taking proper precautions to prepare your path for success, then this could be when you begin to reap the rich rewards you so definitely deserve. And about time too! On the other hand, if you've been muddling along, relying on others and covering up your

WHAT 1992 HAS IN STORE FOR YOU

troubled tracks, then this could be when everything comes to light and lands you in a pretty pickle. Watch out!

Even if you've got nowt to worry about, try not to become so embroiled in professional pursuits that your nearest and dearest feel they've been put on the back burner or even utterly ignored. They'll soon let you know how they feel if you do!

The early part of the year looks grand if you earn your living from creative, artistic or enjoyable enterprises, especially if you act the entrepreneur and sell your talents to the highest bidder. After October, dealings with colleagues and clients will go from strength to strength, helped by your methodical and meticulous approach.

As a Taurean you like to stick to the true, tried and tested, but by now you should slowly be revising, reconsidering and re-evaluating your view of the world, ready to make radical changes that will have an important influence over your professional progress. Keep an open mind at all times!

YOUR DAY-BY-DAY GUIDE TO 1992

JANUARY

WEDNESDAY, 1st. Start this glorious New Year as you mean to go on, and make sure everyone you care for most knows just how much they mean to you. An intimate affair will certainly set out on a sensationally sizzling and superbly sensual foot as you make the most of your bank holiday rest. Whilst you're on such good terms with the people in your life, why not tackle a few pecuniary problems threatening to divide you? With today's spirit of compromise, you'll quickly arrive at an amicable agreement.

THURSDAY, 2nd. You realise only too well as 1992 gets gradually under way that life is what you make it, and you have every intention of making this a truly marvellous year! Colleagues impressed with your vision and audacious enthusiasm will egg you on, but are you sure you haven't overstepped the bounds of simple good sense? Don't instigate a complex plan designed to take you way beyond your current limits until you've taken a closer look at the facts and figures. Maybe you need to be a tiny bit more realistic?

FRIDAY, 3rd. There are tricky and touchy intimate topics you may normally shy away from, so make the most of Friday's terrifically tactful stars. It's so much easier now to put even the most private and personal feelings into words that are calculated to get through. Seize the chance for a heart-to-heart with the love of your life, or a spot of straight talking with someone you've been secretly sparring with. A few well-chosen words will solve the most perplexing problem today.

SATURDAY, 4th. It's the grand global perspective that occupies your entire outlook Saturday as the Capricorn New Moon sets you out on the New Year with a very enlightened, ethical and moral attitude. In many areas you see this as a make-or-break annum, whether it's a private aim or the political or ecological fate of international affairs that concerns you. Resolve to do your bit, however small, to make this a better world for all.

SUNDAY, 5th. If you cling to out-dated concepts about the fundamental principles of life you'll be in for some shocks and surprises. The heavens demand a quantum leap in your understanding of religious, philosophical or spiritual ideals. So fling open the windows of your mind and admit that you may not have all the answers, although through tolerance you'll learn much. Pay especial attention to comments on international affairs or ethical issues made by a youngster. They may not have much experience, but their innocent and unsophisticated approach will be like a breath of fresh air.

MONDAY, 6th. Whether you're ready to climb to the professional peak or still waiting to set foot on the first rung of success, the heavenly host brings the promise of pleasing progress as kindly Venus pulls out all the stops to make your path smoother and sweeter. It's a wonderful Monday to meet with folk who can give you a career boost, as you have the winning ways and charismatic charm required to win people round to your side now.

TUESDAY, 7th. You're filled to the idealistic brim with hope for the future, but it's not at all easy keeping your eye on a realistic target or ensuring that your ideals are more than merely pie in the sky. Maybe you're wasting your efforts today trying to establish a strictly logical foundation for your beliefs and convictions, for some things must be simply accepted as a matter of faith and trust. If you're all at sea over your idealistic stand on certain issues, talk to someone whose intellect and moral rectitude your respect.

WEDNESDAY, 8th. You've made a pretty impressive start on your year so far, and as a result there are petty jealousies and envious attacks from folk who really should know better. Keep your every action and intention totally open and above board, even if your rivals attempt to hit below the belt, for it makes no sense at all to store up ammunition for others to use against you.

THURSDAY, 9th. The pace in the world at large as well as your own private life is hotting up, aided by the energetic action of Mars marching into Capricorn. Ideals and dogmas you've always accepted without question due to the weight of tradition are no longer adequate as you see the need to think things through for yourself. If folk around seem reluctant to discuss abstract and ethical issues, don't stop at the first refusal, but insist on airing your views. Folk will respect your integrity in sticking to your philosophical, religious or spiritual guns, but don't allow intolerance to spoil your respectable record.

FRIDAY, 10th. Inquisitive wee Mercury's attracted by all the noise and joins mighty Mars in your horoscopic house of intellectual affairs Friday. Notions you've been nursing without quite knowing how to word them can be easily expressed now, helping you to persuade others to follow your lead. Whilst you have such an open mind and interested attitude, why not plan a holiday or trip to somewhere with very different customs and beliefs? You'll relish the chance to learn something more about the world at large.

SATURDAY, 11th. Spiritual satisfaction and intellectual understanding are top of the astral agenda now, as you feel drawn to delve into the more mysterious and marvellously magical areas of your world, searching for truth and beauty. You may not be accustomed to undertaking ethical inquiries or religious ruminations, but do take some time simply to consider your position on various issues. Let your intuition take the lead, for logic alone is not enough to solve some of the sticky problems facing you and the world in general.

SUNDAY, 12th. Sensational starluck showers down this Sunday as generous Jupiterian vibes are enhanced and encouraged by electrifying Uranus. Tune yourself in to the youth culture, get informed on scientific innovations and technological advances, and you're sure to see plenty of ways to advance your personal interests as well. For the moment you may be better off keeping any interest in the fresh spirit sweeping through the land purely theoretical rather than practical, for there's also an extravagant aura around today that could lead you to commit more cash than you can afford.

MONDAY, 13th. There's a powerful pairing between the Sun and Pluto this Monday, gently but insistently urging you to overhaul your one-to-one affairs and eliminate any bones of contention or unclear issues. Don't hesitate to dig really deeply into any tender or delicate topics that are normally kept under wraps, as you have a chance now to rid yourself of anything eating away at the fond foundations of your togetherness. Solo Bulls should concentrate on fiscal affairs, for there may be hidden faults and failings that are better aired than ignored.

TUESDAY, 14th. It's one of those days when you'll need all of your Taurean patience, as every step you make seems to take you straight into a brick wall of official indifference or distracting and discouraging delays. You tend to feel any problems you encounter are aimed at you as a personal insult, but that's an overreaction. You'll do your reputation more good by showing patient perseverance now than by railing irritably against anyone or anything standing in your way. A frustrating Tuesday.

WEDNESDAY, 15th. If you and your other half have tried to turn a blissful blind eye to fundamental strains and stresses in the basic structure of your relationship you'll need to face a few facts now. Mother Moon is in the searing spotlight of powerful Pluto, intensifying even the most ephemeral emotion and picking out any personal problems in high relief. If you're at odds with someone you basically cherish and adore, maybe you should consent to a compromise rather than sticking to your position come hell or high water. Remember, every relationship requires give-and-take if its to work out!

THURSDAY, 16th. You're at your patient, practical and persistent best this Thursday, ready to put in the careful and cautious work required to help you make your mark in the world. This is the perfect time to talk to someone in a position of authority about your pecuniary position and to work out ways of safeguarding your fiscal future. Your sound sense and economic acumen will very favourably impress the powers that be.

FRIDAY, 17th. Well, my friend, you've certainly earned a spot of astral assistance, and Friday's stars shine with a loving and luxurious light that will have you in your seventh heaven if I'm not mistaken! This is a wonderful day to treat yourself to a wee shopping spree to sample the January bargains. You may be a mite indulgent, but after all, you deserve a few treats! Your love life is equally enchanting as amour heads the astral agenda. Just make sure you do your duty before sinking into a sensual sea of pure pleasure!

SATURDAY, 18th. Something's got your goat this Saturday, but it's far from clear just what's made you so quick-tempered, choleric and querulous. The most innocent remark or off-the-cuff comment could get you muttering moodily under your breath, so try to realise others aren't really to blame for your bad temper. Take extra care when travelling or making local errands, and put safety before speed!

SUNDAY, 19th. Have a word with your other half or a well-informed family member about your beliefs and principles Sunday, as they'll appreciate your openness and will help you to deepen your understanding of the world at large. You must eradicate any erroneous or unsubstantiated assumptions that have become a dead weight mentally, as the Full Moon issues an ultimatum for you to buck up your ideas. Youngsters or fun-loving friends have the right idea, so follow their optimistic and enthusiastic lead.

MONDAY, 20th. Solar power reaches a brilliant peak in your personal solar chart this Monday, and for the next month you're in formidable form! It's high time you put the full force of your personal talents and impressive abilities behind your aims and ambitions in life to make the most of your individual potential. Maybe it's time to put in for promotion, or to insist on a more favourable deal from the powers that be? In particular you should be ready to reconsider every established assumption and purely traditional ambition you may have. There are totally original, unorthodox and technologically advanced options open to you now, and this is no time simply to turn your back.

TUESDAY, 21st. Madcap Mercury is being led a merry dance by nebulous Neptune this Tuesday, resulting for you in a day filled with false starts, mental muddles and lines of thought that ultimately lead you into a terrible tangle. Partly the problem lies with your desire to be idealistic above all, and to put practical concerns to one side for a change. It's an admirable attempt, but you very quickly get out of your depth. So long as you accept that your mind's working in an irrational, imaginative and inspirational mode that won't necessarily make sense, you'll be fine.

WEDNESDAY, 22nd. What a fun-loving Bull you are today! There's an invigorating contact between the Moon and Mars urging you to make the most of any leisure and pleasure opportunities coming your way. If your schedule so far holds nothing but dreary duties, it's time you stepped in and inserted a few off-duty extras like a drink after work with your buddies, or extra time playing with your kids. All work and no play makes for a dull Taurean, and it's up to you to rectify the situation!

THURSDAY, 23rd. Now the thrill of Christmas has worn off, any children in your world are beginning to crave new novelties and expensive treats. Or maybe it's you that has an itch to lavish loot on a spot of luxury? I don't mean to be a killjoy, but are you quite sure you can afford an extravagant binge? You must be especially careful if you're planning to use funds you hold in common with someone else. Give common sense a look-in before you part with any significant sums.

FRIDAY, 24th. What a hard-working soul you are! Anyone with you on their team will be thanking their lucky stars this Friday, for although you may not do anything really spectacular, it's the steady way you deal with everything from an office crisis to domestic dramas that marks you out as masterful. You're on a very even keel now, Taurus, and can expect to be appreciated by companions, colleagues and clients alike.

SATURDAY, 25th. The more you can open your mind to artistic and emotional experiences over the coming weeks, the more you'll learn. Visit somewhere new, watch an unusual film or borrow a mind-boggling book now and start expanding your horizon in a rewarding and intriguing way. Saturday's stars stimulate a driving desire to peer far beyond your own personal horizons and to comprehend much more of the many different cultures and belief systems operating in this world. A close personal partner could offer some very insightful ideas on a question of principle.

SUNDAY, 26th. Listen to any ideas your other half may have that are designed to improve the luxury-level in your lives and produce a more appealing parade of pleasures, for they know just what you like and have the affectionate intention of making your day! Anything from a slap-up lunch at a ritzy restaurant to an afternoon spent strolling in the wonderful countryside or imbibing the cultured and classy atmosphere of an up-market art exhibition – whatever they have in mind, you'd be daft not to go along with it!

MONDAY, 27th. The time has come for all-out action, Taurus, for there's a fantastically favourable link-up between lucky Jupiter and go-getting Mars in Monday's marvellous sky. A personal project may show so much promise you feel ready to break into the big time, or maybe a creative idea you've had is ripe for development? Be audacious and adventurous in pushing yourself to the fore today, and you'll meet with a heart-warming and very exhilarating positive response. The ball's in your court, Taurus!

TUESDAY, 28th. I know you've been doing pretty well following your own independent nose lately, but you're in danger of overlooking a superb source of advice and support in your other half, or a professional partner. Talk over your plans with someone you trust and respect and they could well come up with a few pointers that will prove absolutely invaluable. At the very least it'll help reassure you to know the backing's there if you should feel the need in the future.

WEDNESDAY, 29th. You get the galactical green light from Mercury as he skips smartly into your solar house of occupational affairs. Up to mid-February you should arrange for interviews or meetings with folk who can help you to make your mark as you express yourself with such confident assurance and articulate eloquence. For today, however, you must steel yourself for the occasional refusal or blocked application as the stars test your mettle. Don't overreact to anyone coming across as an arrogant autocrat, however intensely their pompous approach may annoy you. A temperamental outburst is unlikely to do your cause much good.

THURSDAY, 30th. It's been quite a week, and it's still only Thursday! You're feeling in need of a break from the practical pressures of life and will benefit enormously from a change of scene if that's a possibility. If a day's outing or even an early holiday is out of the question, at least make sure you arrange for an evening spent far from your everyday anxieties. Maybe a magical movie or good book will do the trick and take you away from it all in your active imagination?

FRIDAY, 31st. You're fascinated by foreign cultures, and feel overwhelmed by a driving desire to sample strange and outlandish pleasures. It could be an amorous encounter with someone from a totally different background getting your imagination going, or a travel documentary on the TV showing the dazzling beauties of an exotic part of the world. Turn your attention to unusual and far-flung delights this Friday. If you're off on a long journey, you can expect plenty in the way of enjoyment and excitement.

FEBRUARY

SATURDAY, 1st. If you were thinking of taking a principled stand on an issue you feel very strongly about today, my advice is to consider very carefully, and then check your facts again before making any kind of public statement. You mean well, and want to act on the highest of spiritual standards or ethical ideals, but you're inclined to fall into every pitfall going, simply through muddle-headed mistakes and unrealistic ideas. It's not like you to be so impractical, but that's your problem today.

SUNDAY, 2nd. If I were you I'd spend your Sunday with your feet up, and surrounded by the creature comforts of home, for there's a super-sensitive sky. Make sure you're occupied with some simple and soothing tasks, for if you let your mind wander you'll soon start to dwell on the events of the week, going over various hurtful remarks or discouraging signs until you've magnified them into major problems. Don't let your anxious imagination get carried away!

MONDAY, 3rd. With many exciting and encouraging astral energies aimed at you from the sign of Aquarius now, you know that one false move could leave you in a very precarious position. Once again ambitions and work seem to be unfulfilling and aimless and it's time for you to state your case to your superiors if you wish to transform and alter your present career condition. Breathe fresh life into your ambitions, Taurus.

TUESDAY, 4th. What a terrific Tuesday! Where leisure and pleasure are concerned you couldn't ask for a more auspicious outlook, whether you're looking for love or keen to promote a pet pastime. It's the perfect time to expand your activities and look for enjoyable openings beyond your usual round. Talks aimed at improving your status at work or in a private capacity could run into a brick wall, but if you hold your ground you'll impress folk with your dogged determination and they may gradually come around to your position.

WEDNESDAY, 5th. Charitable appeals that touched you to the core over Christmas are once more uppermost in your mind as you ponder the plight of folk worse off than you. Chat to your many caring and compassionate chums and see if you can't organise a fund-raising event or donate some time to a local cause. The problems may seem far too overwhelming for you to tackle on your tod, but a joint effort can certainly help make a kindhearted impact.

THURSDAY, 6th. A most unassuming little aspect makes today a rather pleasurable and quietly enjoyable one. Social activities, a cultured outing or maybe a romantic dinner – whatever is your indulgence today will make you feel on top of the world and ready to share your happiness with all and sundry. As you will be inclined to feel a little lazy, don't take on too much.

FRIDAY, 7th. Your much-loved traditions and cherished conservative values could be unexpectedly overturned by the ruthlessly radical combination of your ruler, velvet Venus, with rebellious Uranus today. It's an experimental opportunity to dabble with art forms, ethical ideas or political principles you've always dismissed as far too unorthodox before, so make the most of your free-thinking attitude. Don't commit yourself to a particular position whilst your mood is so erratic and experimental.

SATURDAY, 8th. Reading a book, watching a TV programme or browsing through holiday brochures Saturday could set you off on a philosophical or spiritual journey that gets you pondering on the ways of the world and determined to discover more about the deeper and serious side of life. Let your mind escape its everyday chains and wander where it will. At the same time, there are unresolved stresses and strains building up in your one-to-one affairs, so rather than turning a blind eye and hoping you can avoid facing facts, take urgent action now. A straightforward and decisive approach to partnership problems is your best bet now.

SUNDAY, 9th. Self-indulgence of the most deliciously delightful sort is written large in your Sunday sky, so prepare to pamper yourself! You certainly haven't the out-going energy to do much more than tuck into a lavish lunch and potter peacefully around the house, so why force yourself to do anything more active? You need a good rest, and this is your chance to unwind completely.

MONDAY, 10th. Monday morning blues are a distinct and depressing possibility today as chilly Saturnine vibes set the strict seal on your astral outlook. There's nothing for it but to keep your nose to the grindstone, do your duty and wait for any entrenched opposition gradually to give way. Things look much darker than they really are, as you tend to take any obstacle far too much to heart.

TUESDAY, 11th. Head for the hills if you can Tuesday, as the change'll do you the world of good. A joyful jaunt or pleasant promenade to a place of historical or cultural interest could combine entertainment and education by introducing you to fascinating facts or a new train of thought. An evening class, study group or meeting with someone from another clime will be fun.

WEDNESDAY, 12th. There's a very potent and potentially polemical planetary line-up this Wednesday as the Sun and Mercury clash with Pluto, and Venus does her level best to smooth things over. There are certain differences of opinion between you and a close personal partner that are becoming more entrenched and intransigent by the minute. You both feel a point of principle is at stake and refuse to budge an inch, and quite honestly that's a stalemate situation that could last a very long time if you're not careful. Allow the spirit of compromise and consultation to creep into a tense and temperamental situation and you won't regret it.

THURSDAY, 13th. Steady as you go, Taurus! This is a splendidly settled and superbly stable day when you can really get on with the everyday errands that are so important to keep things running smoothly. If you want to make sure you're in the boss's good books, now's the time to put in a spot of overtime or to tackle a task requiring endless patience and persistence. Don't expect immediate rewards, but you'll do your overall prospects plenty of good.

FRIDAY, 14th. Your Valentine vibes are distinctly prosaic as you get on with your daily duties and refuse steadfastly to be swept off your feet, however many cute cards, beautiful bouquets or mysterious messages of amour come your way. Being a practical wee Bull you're not about to let mere romance interfere with life's essentials, and that's just why you're so loved and admired!

SATURDAY, 15th. Beware of getting a bee in your bonnet under Saturday's fanatical sky, for you're inclined to let ideas take a hold and push out all other thoughts. Maybe you've decided radically to improve your entire lifestyle or to get a few things straight with your other half? It's a fine time to insist on some straight talking, but don't get too annoyed if less dedicated folk wander from the point every so often.

SUNDAY, 16th. As Mercury trots gaily into your solar house of future hopes and wishes, so you're overcome with delightful dreams and fond fantasies about the happy and harmonious world that should be within your reach. Seek inspiration and advice from friends and companions in the coming few weeks rather than trying to think things through on your tod. After all, what are friends for? This is a delightful time for all group activities and social meetings.

MONDAY, 17th. Are domestic duties turning into a millstone around your neck, or are professional obligations perhaps weighing you down? You'll feel distinctly drained, depressed and discouraged by Monday's mournful mood if you take every petty problem or irritating obstacle too much to heart. By taking things one step at a time you'll find you're making much better headway than you thought.

TUESDAY, 18th. Today's domestic Full Moon shows up the dusty corners and emotional inconsistencies cluttering up your home life. An early spring clean is what's required if you and your kinfolk are to be liberated from outdated and obsolete attitudes. This is also the beginning of a very progressive period indeed on the public front as both Mars and Venus back you to the harmonious hilt in any bid for the big time. You can count on your own charisma in pursuing every ambitious aim now.

WEDNESDAY, 19th. The loving link-up of Venus and Mars right at the summit of your solar chart continues to dominate the celestial scene, and this is a marvellous opportunity to make a move designed to improve your prospects. Talk to potential backers, apply for prestigious posts and generally use your charms on anyone in a position of power. You're impressively attractive now! There's also an important astral emphasis on your future hopes and wishes as the Sun slips into Pisces for a spell. Use the weeks ahead to get involved in anything that puts your most idealistic and humanitarian ideals to the forefront.

THURSDAY, 20th. An amorous innuendo or loving look from someone you work with or meet via your business could set your wee heart fluttering this Thursday. Or perhaps you encounter customers, clients or colleagues who show a genuine interest in helping you to make the grade. Don't hesitate to exploit the goodwill you've created in the past in order to improve your personal professional prospects. A delightful day when you feel wanted wherever you wander!

FRIDAY, 21st. An unexciting, quietly constructive sort of day when you should keep your nose to the grindstone and make the most of this chance to get a few routine errands and prosaic tasks out of the way. Make yourself a methodical list of all you have to do and systematically cross things off as you do them. To an outside observer it may look dull, but you know there's a glorious glow of satisfaction at seeing that long line of tidy ticks!

SATURDAY, 22nd. A wild-eyed youngster or excitable friend will be egging you on this Saturday, as they consider it's high time to break out of a routine rut and sample much more adventurous pleasures. You're not normally keen on an unplanned outing or impromptu experiment, but you'll be tempted today to throw in your lot with the optimistic innovators of this world. Just don't go to an unrealistic extreme and commit yourself to a scheme with no practical properties at all.

SUNDAY, 23rd. You've put your heart and soul into making the most of last week's enviable astral opportunities, and it seems to me you've pushed yourself just a little bit too hard. You need to unwind but some folk have a different idea, loading you down with overtime from the office, or domestic duties you could really do without. Don't be a martyr and wind up tired and temperamental. You have to draw the line somewhere.

MONDAY, 24th. Potent Pluto pauses and starts a distracting detour, forcing you and a loved one or a professional partner to go back over old ground to make absolutely sure there are no loose ends in your understanding. A bout of jealousy may well come between you and someone around you. You will undoubtedly be tempted to let the little green-eyed monster take you over completely which will do neither you nor your partner any good at all, so keep your cool and avoid an obsessive attitude.

TUESDAY, 25th. Your solid bovine feet are planted firmly on the ground, but your head is up in the air this Tuesday as you dabble with all kinds of innovative, original and downright unorthodox ideas. Your personal principles in everything from an environmental issue to political pronouncements or a scientific advance are under examination, and you may well feel it's time to make a few changes. Listen to a well-informed friend or up-to-the-minute adviser and they'll help you to sort out your true personal position. How exciting!

WEDNESDAY, 26th. Poetic and prophetic pronouncements flow from your inspired lips this Wednesday, giving the lie to your more prosaic and pedantic image. Mentally you're in tune with the spiritual certainties and ethical ideals that can make this such a marvellous world for all. Speak up about your vision for a fantastic future and you'll soon win round even the most hard-headed materialist.

THURSDAY, 27th. Purely practical concerns continue to take a back seat in your life as your thoughts and feelings focus on a much more elevated plane. You may not be able to assess certain ideals and principles on an intellectual level, so apply your intuition to a particular issue or problem and let your heart have a say. You know the difference between right and wrong now without having to figure it out in terms of mere logic.

FRIDAY, 28th. What a mental marvel! If you're normally tongue-tied, seize your chance this Friday to speak up on an issue you feel very strongly about. Or perhaps you can speak for your other half or a fearful friend who may be too shy? Anyone laying a false trail or trying to mislead you with superficial points or bland admonishments will be in for a shock as you cut instantly through any waffle and get to the crux of the matter. Put your intellectual expertise at the disposal of a cherished cause or campaign, but don't ignore personal problems that will benefit from a spot of shrewd analysis.

SATURDAY, 29th. Socially you're in sparkling form, ready to celebrate this Leap Year Day in superb style with fun-loving friends, cheerful children or a rapturous romantic rendezvous. There's a fly in the ointment when it comes to your professional standing and career ambitions, as benefits you thought were owing seem delayed or even diverted. Insist on what's truly your due, going back to any written agreements and explaining matters with painstaking and even pedantic precision. A sensible, step-by-step approach will help you win through.

MARCH

SUNDAY, 1st. This is supposed to be a day of rest, but as far as you're concerned it's just one thing after another as you grapple with domestic duties and overtime obligations at work. You're absolutely determined not to let the side down, whether you're struggling to get the garden dug or want to file an important report in the morning, but the strain will begin to tell if you're not careful. Make sure you treat yourself to at least a few minutes with your feet up!

MONDAY, 2nd. A beautifully social aspect linking Venus with the Moon should leave you feeling nicely contented and a little bit loving too. Women friends or female bosses are good for you and could be the key to professional advancement in some way. Listen to all feminine words as they are pearls of wisdom. Your public image is enchantingly enhanced, so you can be sure of a warm response from anyone you approach.

TUESDAY, 3rd. From today you're astrally embarked on a pleasurably peaceful period of quiet contemplation and reserved reticence. You're not willing to open your mouth any more than is absolutely necessary, for your attention is entranced by an inner world of mystery and imagination. Until early April your ability to think things through on a rational level is undermined as intuitive and instinctive impulses rise reflectively to the surface of your mind.

WEDNESDAY, 4th. Wednesday's sensitive sky marks an important turning point in your plans for your future as the New Moon reminds you that it's time to decide once and for all exactly how your overall objectives can be realistically accomplished. You should look especially closely at any humanitarian, spiritual or political ideals you've been nursing, for not only are you poised on the brink of personal progress but you also have the potential to bring about real benefits and reforms on behalf of others. Maybe it's time you joined an idealistic society or palled up with other concerned comrades?

THURSDAY, 5th. There are experienced acquaintances and well-informed friends in your life you should talk to about a partnership problem. You may prefer to keep certain details private, but if you give them the gist they'll soon deduce the nub of the problem and proffer some very reassuring and pertinent advice. Make discreet enquiries rather than trying to struggle on in the dark.

FRIDAY, 6th. I know you're reputed to be as strong as an ox, but even your broad shoulders will begin to creak and groan under the burdens you're expected to bear today. It's flattering to be entrusted with so much responsibility and sheer hard work, and if you acquit yourself well there could be promotion in the offing. Be as efficient, methodical and systematic as possible in all your actions now, and you can accomplish titanic challenges and lay some very firm foundations for future success. You'll certainly earn every advance, however!

SATURDAY, 7th. There's a faithful band of friends you wouldn't dream of deserting, Taurus, but isn't it time you added to their number? You'll all benefit from some fresh blood to help liven up your social circle, especially if you consider teaming up with a controversial figure or up-to-the-minute companion. A radical campaign to bring about far-reaching reforms will capture your attention and should be given some solid Taurean support.

SUNDAY, 8th. Personal principles dominate Sunday's celestial scene, and if you're wise you'll take the opportunity to ponder your beliefs and contemplate your creed. Are you living according to your most elevated ideals? Or are there a few areas where you could act with more kindness and compassion? A small gesture of goodwill today will go a long way to ensuring peace of mind and an easy conscience.

MONDAY, 9th. You may be quite content to carry on calmly with your weekly chores on your own, but let's face it, it's a lot more fun to share things with a band of buddies or party of pals. Give your sociable side full rein, even if you're just getting on with your usual errands, for a cheery greeting or even a joint effort will make the day go with a swing. If you can, spend the evening in congenial company and ensure an enjoyable end to your day.

TUESDAY, 10th. Perhaps you overdid yourself yesterday? Or have you simply run out of steam? At all events, you're just not at your most dynamic today, and feel far more inclined to stretch out on a nice comfy sofa than to tackle anything more adventurous. There could be some opportunist officials trying to pull a fast one simply because of your *laissez-faire* attitude, so try not to agree to all kinds of extra duties simply to keep the peace.

WEDNESDAY, 11th. What more could a down-to-earth Bull wish for than such a quietly constructive and blissfully busy day? Your every effort, whilst not leading to unexpected or exceptional gains, will prove highly efficient and effective. This is a fine time to tie up loose ends and generally get your personal and public affairs in apple-pie order. Balance your cheque book, settle your accounts and get up to date with your work reports. It all makes excellent sense.

THURSDAY, 12th. Are you receiving the financial remuneration your efforts really deserve? And is the respect due to your public position forthcoming? Even if the answer's a resounding 'no', Thursday brings distinct improvements so long as you make the effort to point out where you feel you're worth more. Don't back down simply because you hate to make waves – a diplomatic and discreet reminder of your true value to anyone employing your abilities and aptitudes will yield rich rewards now.

FRIDAY, 13th. Taureans with a superstitious streak need have no fear, for today's celestial scene is jam-packed with planetary promise. You very own Venus sashays sweetly into Pisces, ushering in a time of amorous enjoyment and friendly fun when you can expect your personal popularity to soar right through the roof! You're also handed an astral opportunity to dig deeply into a personal problem, perhaps with the aid of a perceptive pal, and to uncover a cure for emotional or amorous ailment.

SATURDAY, 14th. Don't let the chilly March winds cool your sociable spirit, for it's party time for all swinging sexy and sociable Taureans! You're in the mood for a spot of sociable merrymaking and congenial company, so don't pine away on your own when a friendly chat with a chum is just a phone call away. Take an active and alert interest in anyone you encounter Saturday, and they'll repay your effort with a warm welcome and cordial company.

SUNDAY, 15th. Did you overstep the mark a wee bit in yesterday's revels? Or perhaps you clean forgot certain weekend duties you had lined up? Well, there's no ignoring them now, as peevish family members or your own prickly conscience remind you of the long list of tasks awaiting. There's nothing to be gained from complaining and hoping they'll go away if you ignore them – this is one Sunday you can't spare the time simply to put your feet up.

MONDAY, 16th. There's a family fracas or relationship row in the air this Monday, so if you know you're walking into an emotional minefield, go carefully rather than rush in like a bull in a china shop. There's a need to be very sensitive towards other folks' feelings, otherwise you'll end up hurting or upsetting people and you'll have to clear up the mess. Go easy!

TUESDAY, 17th. Mentally you're not at your most alert and incisive just now, and from today you're apt to get into even more of a muddle as you try to sort out some very peculiar notions. Even the simplest message could get garbled if you rely simply on your memory now and up until 10 April, so carry a notebook around with you or ask someone to back you up on any really important issues. Postal delays and diversions could lead to your getting only half the picture.

WEDNESDAY, 18th. Anyone coming across as even the teensiest bit autocratic or arrogant this warlike Wednesday will quickly find they've got a bellowing, belligerent and bellicose Bull on their hands! Don't get your horns locked into a power struggle with no hope of a solution, for your stubborn streak could so easily lead you down a blind alley today. Today also brings a beautiful Full Moon to light your life and help you cast out any creative catastrophes or romantic red herrings in order to develop your true potential. Don't hold on to past successes, for they'll block the flow of future inspirations.

THURSDAY, 19th. Once you get up momentum, Taurus, you have great difficulty reining yourself in, and that's the problem Thursday as you get carried away by your legendary love of luxury until you're teetering on the edge of extravagant excess. Fun-loving friends could egg you on to spend far more time and cash than you can really afford, or maybe you fancy a flutter and see no reason to quit whilst you're ahead? Moderation is your best policy on this opulently enjoyable day!

FRIDAY, 20th. The spring equinox today dawns for you with a softly sentimental, sensitive and secretive light. You're just not ready to launch yourself in an all-out attack on the world, preferring to ponder your plans in peace and quiet. You have a marvellous month ahead to commune with your inner world and get in touch with your dearest dreams as a way of recharging your batteries in readiness for the superb summer ahead!

SATURDAY, 21st. There's a happy hint of spring in your heart today, for the Moon and Venus cook up a little sparkling stellar magic just for you! Seek out a charming companion to share your taste in the good life, treat your other half to a night out on the town or buy in a few tasty treats and make a night of it in the comfort of your own home. A solitary and spartan Saturday is the last thing on your list!

SUNDAY, 22nd. As Mother Moon and macho Mars snap irritably at each other across the heavens, so you and yours are caught in the cantankerous cross-fire. Petty points and irritating details grate on your nerves and set up irascible eddies of anger swirling around your normally sweet-tempered abode. Try to let off steam by tackling a demanding task or strenuous spot of housework and you'll feel much more affable.

MONDAY, 23rd. What a marvellous Monday! Fretful fires have all burned out, leaving you with a charmingly sweet and reasonable outlook on life. In fact you're super-sensitive to folk with personal problems of their own, and will readily put your own interests in second place if it means helping someone who's down. You're not in it for the glory, but you will earn plenty of heartfelt gratitude from anyone receiving your kindness and consideration now.

TUESDAY, 24th. We all like to be popular, but aren't you taking your bid to stay in a pal's good books just a little too far? Remember that friendship is something that can't be bought, and a pal who's constantly calling on your generosity to help them out of a fiscal scrape may be taking you for an expensive ride. Keep your charitable impulses within sensible bounds this Tuesday or you could live to regret it.

WEDNESDAY, 25th. Working Bulls or Taureans with a taste for personal power and prestige should take a more active and assertive part in pursuing their aims and ambitions this Wednesday. Make sure a few of the influential officials in your line of work notice your dedication to duty and you'll store up plenty of brownie points on your own behalf! In particular you should press for a better fiscal deal from the powers that be.

THURSDAY, 26th. When the powerful Sun combines forces with madcap Mercury in your solar house of imagination and dreams you can expect your vivid imagination and fantastic fund of fantasy to take wings and soar far above merely mundane matters. An intuitive hunch concerning your most spiritual ideals should be thought through in depth since you're at your inspired and instinctive best now. Steer clear of external distractions as much as possible.

FRIDAY, 27th. International affairs may impinge on your awareness this Friday as you realise even events far away can have an ultimate effect on your own life. Or perhaps contact with someone from overseas will set you thinking along cultural and idealistic lines. It's most illuminating to look at things in your own personal life from a fresh perspective too, helping you to realise just how much certain people and places really mean to you. You're in a reflective, mellow mood, Taurus.

SATURDAY, 28th. No one's trying to deny the lasting value of certain traditional institutions or ideals, but isn't it time you bucked your ideas up just a tiny bit? Listen to a modernistic pal and at least find out what up-to-the-minute folk are thinking nowadays. You could have a very pleasant surprise! Socially you're all set to sparkle as Mars marches into your horoscopic house of friendship and group activities. You're no longer content to take a back seat in all social and organised affairs, so speak out and take action on your own individual ideas. You'll soon win a keen following!

SUNDAY, 29th. Celestial harmony between velvet Venus and nectarine Neptune plays a very sweet tune in your world this Sunday. Without quite knowing how or why, you're enraptured by a fond friend, or enmeshed in the magic of a doctrine you find full of kindness, compassion and consideration. This is a marvellous opportunity to dwell on the softer side of life, whether you're of a religious turn of mind or more interested in the pleasures of the flesh!

MONDAY, 30th. A mad social whirl envelops you and carries you off on the pursuit of pleasure this Monday, despite the long list of unexciting errands you were expecting. It's all eminently enjoyable, but you could completely lose track of any prosaic plans you'd made in the midst of all the excitement. Make sure you have a few tranquil moments to yourself to check your diary, and make sure you don't miss any important appointments.

TUESDAY, 31st. As far as you're concerned, you did your duty yesterday and have no intention of sacrificing any more of your precious leisure and pleasure time for anything dull and dreary. Fun is all you seek now, making the convivial company of children especially enjoyable, and placing you at the centre of any sparkling social scene. Just don't let an over-enthusiastic pal persuade you to part with more cash than you can afford on a wild gamble that may or may not pay off!

APRIL

WEDNESDAY, 1st. April Fools' Day need hold no fears, for the heavens are in a harmonious and very helpful mood, especially where your love life or other personal partnerships are concerned. If you and your other half are drifting apart, now's the time to step in and stop the rot. There may be delicate and sensitive issues tobe addressed, but you know very well you'll get nowhere by simply sticking your head in the sand. Face up to the fundamental facts about your relationships and set about patching up any flaws or failings.

THURSDAY, 2nd. I suggest this Thursday should be made as restful and relaxing as possible. If you can, get far away from the hustle and bustle of ordinary life. A retreat or journey to a peaceful place will bring out the very essence of tranquillity for you. This is a time to look deeply into your spiritual values and understanding of life.

FRIDAY, 3rd. Mischievous Mercury slips backwards into Pisces for a short spell, enhancing your overall sensitivity to the true feelings of your friends. But at the same time you're so acutely aware of every unspoken thought and insinuated meaning you find even everyday conversation a bit of a trial. Try to be a wee bit more methodical and moderate in your thinking. Today's New Moon also stimulates your incredible intuition, as on a deep, inner level you realise it's time you renewed many of your dreams and desires. An act of kindness may serve to set you on a more fulfilling personal path.

SATURDAY, 4th. Hold your horses, Taurus! I know it's a splendid spring-time Saturday, but aren't you planning to pack in just a bit too much sumptuous socialising? Maybe you've been listening to avid youngsters with no sense of timing or economy, or is it an enthusiastic pal who's urged you to put all traces of common sense to one side? By all means enjoy yourself to the full now you have so much exuberant energy, but don't feel obliged to push yourself beyond sensible limits just to keep up a congenial appearance.

SUNDAY, 5th. As you take stock of your state of health and the condition of your purse or wallet this Sunday, you'll be thanking your lucky stars that you're a sensible Bull and knew where to draw the line yesterday. Even if you went a wee bit over the top, you've a chance now to assess the damage and prepare a plan to put your financial and physical world back on to some firm foundations. A superbly sane, settled and sensible Sunday.

MONDAY, 6th. You may not know precisely what you want to say to the people you encounter Monday, but you only have to open your mouth to be sure of charming the socks off them! There's an eloquent and affable association of Mercury and Venus imbuing you with all the eloquence required to win round enemies and bring firm friends even closer, so make the most of this perfectly pleasant and peaceable day.

TUESDAY, 7th. Just as if you've been struck by lightning, you're electrified by a revelation this Tuesday as sudden notions and totally unexpected inspirations flood unannounced into your startled mind! All at once your humanitarian and spiritual ideals are crystal clear and all you want to do is show folk the error of their ways. Temper your teachings with plenty of tact and tolerance or you'll simply stir up entrenched opposition. Today also sees the ecstatic entry of Venus into one of the most private and personal areas of your chart, making you realise just how many blessings you have to count, whatever your material situation. Until early May you should set about sharing your good fortune, even if all you have to give is a cheery smile or spot of sensitive sympathy.

WEDNESDAY, 8th. What a wistful Wednesday! You're just not sure what you feel now, much less what you think about certain pressing issues and controversial topics, and if I were you I wouldn't make any rash public statements. Anyone with any wit at all could persuade you to part with cash or give public support to a cause you don't really care for, simply because they come up with a convincing sob-story or play on your sympathies. This is no time to take action, since your view is obscured by a tricky Neptunian mist.

THURSDAY, 9th. At last you have some chance of getting your message across without running into endless misunderstandings and mistakes. The peripatetic planet of communications is back on course, and you're able to concentrate properly once more. You've a welcome week now to speak to puzzled pals and confused companions so as to correct any false impression you've given over the past few weeks.

FRIDAY, 10th. Don't rely exclusively on your intuition this Friday, even if it has served you superbly well in the past. For today's sky holds a misleading message that could result in a myriad misunderstandings and muddles whenever you try to express emotional issues in mere words. You should also be extra careful when agreeing to appointments, interviews or meetings for you could so easily double-book yourself if you don't stay alert and on the ball. Try to keep things simple.

SATURDAY, 11th. You're such a soft-hearted and sympathetic soul Saturday, and if you're not very careful your loved ones could twist you right round their little fingers just by smiling sweetly! Happily they're not out to take you for a ride, for they're equally enamoured of your agreeable and appealing aura! It's a wonderful day to put on your comfiest carpet slippers and spend a cosy evening with the folk at home, as domestic bliss is the astral order of the day. Mmmmmm!

SUNDAY, 12th. You had such a lovely time Saturday you see no reason to call a halt, and neither do I! Immerse yourself right up to your Taurean neck in the calm, quiet and contemplative pleasures of a day spent far from the hustle and bustle. Maybe you can take a trip out into the country to help recharge your emotional batteries? Whatever gives you the most profound sense of peace, that's what you should be doing today.

MONDAY, 13th. I know I told you to recharge your batteries, but it seems to me you've overdone it a wee bit on the fun-filled voltage! You're overflowing with an exuberant zest for life that'll soon make you the sparkling star of any gregarious gathering. Watch out for a yen to improve your fortunes by gambling, for you're a touch too optimistic now to assess the realistic risks.

TUESDAY, 14th. You're faced now with a marvellous month when your meditative mentality makes you shy away from too many extrovert engagements and prefer the quiet company of your own imagination. That's marvellous for daydreams, but not so good when you have to tackle the endless petty problems and day-to-day decisions facing us all. Remember that you're just not at your most lucid and logical, and avoid making any really important choices whilst you're in such a mental fog.

WEDNESDAY, 15th. You're trying so hard to put your all into the daily demands made on your energies, but you must know where to draw the line. Trying to take too much on to your broad shoulders will only undermine your health and strength in the long run, so the minute you begin to feel the strain you should call a wee halt. Look after yourself, Taurus!

THURSDAY, 16th. Does your approach to health care involve lots of tasty treats and a somnolent spell stretched out on the sofa? That's all very well, but you know your body needs a spot more physical exercise and discipline than that to keep in tip-top shape. Dietary indulgence is your particular bugbear, and today you need to be more than usually vigilant or you'll find your hand in that biscuit tin before you realise it!

FRIDAY, 17th. Far-reaching changes and useful alterations at work MUST be made if you are to reach the happy heights of job-satisfaction and personal fulfilment that seem to be eluding you at present. You cannot go on in the way you have been doing, so take the bull by the horns and prepare to take action professionally. Health practices you know aren't doing you any good must also be curtailed.

SATURDAY, 18th. Are you tired of always following the lead of a forthright friend when it comes to setting your social circle in a spin? Well, now's your chance to pip them to the party-going post by throwing an impromptu affair yourself, or organising an outing arranged along laughter-loving lines chosen by you. Prepare to enjoy yourself to the full this Saturday, Taureans!

SUNDAY, 19th. The glorious golden glow of the majestic Sun honours your very own sign with his proud and playful presence for a whole month, starting on this unforgettable Easter Day. Self-expression takes the top of your astral agenda now you have the courage of your convictions and also the self-confidence to push yourself to the fore. If you feel folk have been ignoring you or consigning you to the back benches, now's your chance to insist on the admiration, adulation and applause you so richly deserve!

MONDAY, 20th. Take advantage of the holiday today to ponder your principles and search for spiritual truth, for you're now entering a very perplexing period when you're prone to confusion. Right up until September you'll need to be extra-careful over just what you choose to believe, for you're susceptible to false prophets and idealistic idiots. Ask a pal with very decided views to illuminate some of the more unorthodox viewpoints today, and they'll help to clarify a very murky scene.

TUESDAY, 21st. Just like Neptune, Uranus had decided to take a detour, taking all settled certainty in your life with him in the process! Certain modern developments on the political, ecological or religious stage seem all at once to be too confusing for words, so don't worry too much if you just can't make sense of them. The picture will eventually come clear. An impassioned plea from a favourite friend sets you on fire with a desire to fight for what is right in the world. Anything from a local scandal to more far-reaching affairs takes on a personal significance when you consider the moral aspects of the problem. Tackle things with sensitivity and sympathy, as an all-out attack will only produce resistance. On the purely practical level, your affairs are proceeding as planned.

WEDNESDAY, 22nd. Your kindly ruler Venus is trapped in a treacherous Neptunian net this wistful Wednesday, and if I were you I'd avoid any sudden actions that could only entangle you more. The trouble is, some folk seem to imply you're keeping your counsel simply because you couldn't care less about a particular problem, and nothing could be further from the tender truth. Don't let unscrupulous folk goad you into doing anything you're not one hundred per cent sure about on this deceptive, disillusioning and discouraging day.

THURSDAY, 23rd. Strive for selfless goals this Thursday and set about being of service to anyone in need, whether it means making an extra effort to help your mum with the shopping, or handing over your spare change for a worthy cause. You'll feel so much better if you make the effort to help others now rather than simply dreaming about kind deeds whilst carrying on as normal. You're super-sensitive to the slightest hint of suffering, and may well need to withdraw from the scene as certain problems simply become too painful to contemplate.

FRIDAY, 24th. Prepare to celebrate, Taurus, for there's such an auspicious astral array this fantastic Friday, you can hardly fail to find something to justify a party! Maybe it's news of a birth in the family, or a pet pastime of yours beginning to blossom – your personal creativity and self-expressive skills have never been more effective and enjoyable. Artistic Bulls may find an admiring audience, so don't hide your creative light under a bashful bushel.

SATURDAY, 25th. Has your other half used you as a doormat for far too long? Or does a business partner tend to take your contribution for granted? Well, now's the perfect time to put your foot down and insist on a much more equitable arrangement. You'll find it's much easier than you expect to get right back to basics in all important personal partnerships, and to eliminate outdated or outworn agreements. Far from leaving you lost and lonely, it allows a much more supportive structure to be built.

SUNDAY, 26th. It's been quite a week, Taurus, and quite honestly you've earned a rest. You're not foolish enough to pass up a chance to put your feet up, take the phone off the hook and generally enjoy a day without external distractions, so go ahead and indulge yourself! If you have family duties to perform, keep them to an absolute minimum.

MONDAY, 27th. You had such a superbly serene Sunday you hardly want to tackle a mundane Monday. There may be unavoidable errands you must run, but just as soon as you can you should treat yourself to a little peace and quiet. Perhaps you can spend the evening pottering peacefully around the garden, or dreaming along with a romantic movie on the TV? Not a good day to attempt an assault on the peaks of professional success!

TUESDAY, 28th. The piercing pleasures of pure passion form an intense emotional undercurrent to Tuesday's events as even everyday situations seem to develop a secretive and stimulating significance. An erotic interlude could be at the root of your delighted and distracted air, or maybe you're about to clinch a financial deal calculated totally to transform your cashflow? Clandestine contacts and inside information provided by a helpful pal could prove extremely useful so long as you act with extreme discretion.

WEDNESDAY, 29th. You're tired of watching your step and weighing every move just like a game of chess, and Wednesday's supercharged stars help you to shake off all restraints. Follow the lead of a forthright friend with a few exciting ideas about living life to the full. It may be tiring keeping up with their punishing pace, but it's well worth the enjoyable effort.

THURSDAY, 30th. Since the very beginning of the year, Jupiter's roundabout route has been causing all kinds of delays and distractions every time you tried to inject a little extra enjoyment into your world. Well, from today you can look for a much more positive response to any creative initiative you make, whether you're looking to found a dynasty or improve your artistic aptitudes. Youngsters who've seemed to be losing their way should begin to get back on the straight and narrow now.

MAY

FRIDAY, 1st. What a smashing way to celebrate May Day! There's good galactical news for all Bulls as your very own Venus makes her entrancing annual entrance into your Sun sign and promises a most enjoyable span. For most of this month you're endowed with an incredible amount of charm, and such superb taste you'll be dressed to kill without even making any effort. Cashflow is also eased by the affable influence of Venus, but don't go and spend any extra income so fast you're left worse off then when you began!

SATURDAY, 2nd. I know we're several months into 1992 already, but as far as you're concerned Saturday brings a glorious sense of beginning afresh, so why not review your resolutions and make a few more? The stimulating light of the New Moon in your Sun sign sets your feet itching for pastures new, whether you're looking for a new personal image or want to tackle far-reaching changes in your circumstances. This is a fine time to make radical personal changes.

SUNDAY, 3rd. Now you have a little spare time to think things through, it seems your imagination has begun to run riot! Perverse notions, crackpot ideas and totally unrealistic ideals fill your head and make you want to preach a new world order based simply on your own very muddled mind. Needless to say, your more way-out ideas aren't likely to meet with much understanding, let alone support, but if you curb your more extreme positions and try to stick to the facts, you could persuade some influential folk to follow you.

MONDAY, 4th. Your bank holiday stars hold such superb promise you should certainly set about packing your day with pleasure aplenty! The only fly in your enjoyable ointment could come from cash constraints forcing you to economise on certain outings and cut short some of your more extravagant ideas. Before you start bemoaning your fate, remember that there's plenty of fun to be had for a very reasonable cost, and enjoyment doesn't HAVE to mean spending like there's no tomorrow!

TUESDAY, 5th. Your solar house of secrets snares fiery Mars Tuesday, and until mid-June you'll need to tread very warily if you're to fulfil your desires without arousing opposition and contention. The harder you try to push yourself into the limelight of life, the more folk will misunderstand your true motives, so play a waiting game and lie low a wee while. Today also brings a fantastically fortunate contact between Venus and Jupiter, promising plenty of luck where both love and loot are concerned!

WEDNESDAY, 6th. Charm oozes effortlessly from every attractive pore under Wednesday's affectionate sky, so prepare to make the most of your personal appeal, Taurus! Whether chatting to a neighbour or attending a local gathering, you're ready to pour affable oil on to troubled waters, so you can expect your diplomatic services to be in delightful demand. You're not too interested in anything too demanding or depressing, preferring the pleasant give-and-take of a congenial conversation.

THURSDAY, 7th. Sweetness and light still characterise your astral outlook, so make the most of this enjoyable opportunity to immerse yourself in the superficial interests and sociable comings and goings of neighbourhood affairs. You're not interested in a controversial cause or campaign; you simply leap at any excuse to find out what your neighbours are up to! No one could take offence at your willingness to chat about everything from a pal's troubles to the way a local event has been organised. A pleasantly chatty day.

FRIDAY, 8th. You're not known as one of the world's innovators, but there's a very positive contact between the Sun and forward-looking Uranus today, helping you to see positive benefits from various up-to-the-minute ideas. Don't hesitate to question old conventions and restrictive traditions, for you see clearly now that only good can come of moving with the times. At least, that's the theory, for you're also fearful of abandoning too much. Or perhaps your boss is coming down hard on any attempt to update your image? Don't let a negative reaction stop you, for now's the time to bring yourself up to date.

SATURDAY, 9th. Folk who think you're a mundane materialist will have to think again Saturday as your most elevated and enlightened ideals come to the fore. It's all-important to you now to live up to your personal principles, and to make some kind of public statement about issues you feel are important. The kindness and kind-hearted consideration behind your outlook will shine through and help you to inspire others to follow your noble example.

SUNDAY, 10th. Lunar light is brilliantly boosted by generous Jupiter, promising a day when leisure and pleasure push out all thoughts of your workaday week. It's an excellent opportunity to catch up with the interests and activities of your children if you're a parent. Or maybe you'd rather spend time on a hobby? Creatively speaking you're second to none now, so don't hesitate to tackle an ambitious project.

MONDAY, 11th. Monday's celestial scene sets you off on a popular period when you've an overwhelming urge to communicate your ideas and ensure that you're being understood. You want to be noticed, and can easily overcome any shyness in order to talk to everyone from your neighbour to a complete stranger in the bus queue. Catch up on your correspondence too, for I'll bet there are plenty of people just dying to hear from you.

TUESDAY, 12th. As Pluto vies with the Sun to take control of your life, so you're faced with a showdown in your one-to-one affairs as you struggle to impose your will at the expense of others. Or perhaps it's a personal partner who's playing the arrogant autocrat? Either way you must break the deadlock and rid yourselves of intransigent attitudes that will only keep you stuck. Be ruthless, for half measures just won't do.

WEDNESDAY, 13th. What a wonderfully well-balanced, steadily sensible Wednesday! You can't expect any surprises, but instead have a chance to get up to date with all the everyday errands and daily duties that so often get pushed to one side. You're in an extremely efficient and effective state of mind and can accomplish a great deal simply by taking things one step at a time.

THURSDAY, 14th. Are you normally inclined to play down your vision for the future and look for a safe option when faced with opportunity? Well, put such canny caution behind you today, for this is your big chance to look on the bright side and plan out a golden future for yourself and anyone sharing your dreams. Talk to anyone and everyone about your ideas, whether it's a creative project, an artistic ambition or an economic scheme you want to promote. You're sure to meet with a positive response since you put yourself across with such good-humoured optimism now. A wonderful day for a journey.

FRIDAY, 15th. Romantic raptures and passionate pleasures are still just as powerful and pressing, but you also need to keep a wise weather eye on the practicalities of life, and this difficult dilemma could have you twisting and turning as your common sense battles it out with your emotions. You're not at your most reasonable and rational with this mental conflict going on, so it's not a good day for delicate or important negotiations.

SATURDAY, 16th. From the look of the heavens this is all set to be quite a Saturday, with a quartet of configurations to be considered. The Scorpionic Full Moon makes this a truly transforming time, when relationships in your life that need to change or grow in some way will find that alterations become unavoidable this weekend. This is an excellent time to face the truth in all of your dealings with others. See people as they really are and don't run away from the truth. Where less personal affairs, and abstract points of principle are concerned, your life will flow along much smoother lines, making all overseas contacts and cultural excursions extra-informative and enjoyable. Watch out for a peevish partner out to spoil your fun, and make sure you fulfil any agreements to the letter.

SUNDAY, 17th. If your suspicions have been aroused by the puzzling behaviour of a beloved partner or business associate, why not ask them openly for an explanation? There's no point in beating about the bush when you can clear up your doubts with a few discreet enquiries. You have the perceptive power now to see easily through any excuses or pretexts that don't ring true.

MONDAY, 18th. Mundane Monday, that's my verdict from today's sensible stars! As a down-to-earth Bull you'll relish the chance to catch up with your 'to do' list and to make sure your affairs are in an well-organised state. If you need fiscal backing for a particular goal, now's the time to present your case to legal, economic and professional advisers who'll be only too happy to put you on the right path.

TUESDAY, 19th. It's a good thing you're not prone to too many flights of fancy, for Tuesday's tense and temperamental sky would test the patience of a saint! Close personal partnerships take the brunt of today's suspicious, secretive and spiteful stars, bringing out the worst in any relationship that's in any way rocky. Don't get side-tracked into a slanging match, for by addressing the underlying problem you'll be able to eliminate the root cause of any difficulties between you. A day when feelings run very strongly indeed.

WEDNESDAY, 20th. The Sun bestows his imperial presence on your solar house of wealth and worth from today for a prosperous period when material and spiritual possessions benefit from a much more positive outlook. If your resources require a bit of a boost, now's the time to set about enriching your income, shoring up your self-confidence or investing in more beautiful belongings. Don't be too tradition-bound to follow up an inventive, innovative and ingenious idea striking like a bolt from the blue. It may seem crackpot, but the chances are there's something in it.

THURSDAY, 21st. Mixed mental influences make this a paradoxical day when you won't know if you're coming or going. Spiritually speaking, you're attuned to some pretty elevated ideas, and should set about finding out more to back up your beliefs. When it comes to pushing forward professionally or getting your message across to anyone in authority, it's a very different picture, promising nothing but delay and distraction. Patience will win your day!

FRIDAY, 22nd. Any ill-advised attempt to be even slightly less than honest in your dealings with others now could lead to a very sticky situation indeed. For however cleverly you lay your false trail, it seems others are one devious step ahead of you, and will second-guess even cunning and complex plots. In any close partnerships you must face up to the fundamental facts that underlie any problems, even if it means owning up to painful pointers you've kept hidden even from yourself. Don't be too stubborn to talk things over.

SATURDAY, 23rd. Now before you utter a word this Saturday, you must make sure you've considered your position. It's not that you're about to make a major blunder, but you could easily chatter on about a topic meant to be confidential, or talk so much about trivialities your audience melts away before your eyes. Keep any conversation light, and avoid tackling any subject demanding concentration or rational thought.

SUNDAY, 24th. In your innermost heart you may know you're up to any challenge the world may throw at you, but at the moment you're having trouble getting that confident message across. It's very frustrating to be misjudged and misunderstood, but you won't get anywhere by dwelling on it all day. The chances are you're not making an accurate assessment of the situation anyway, so don't take today's doubts too seriously.

MONDAY, 25th. Thankfully you don't need to force yourself to take up the challenge of making your way in the world this Monday, for you're in no mood for the hustle and bustle. In fact all you crave is a spot of utter peace and tranquillity, so maybe you could potter around your garden or take a serene stroll through the park? It does your peace-loving heart the world of good!

TUESDAY, 26th. Astral arm in affable arm, Mercury and Venus step jauntily into your solar house of economic affairs and self-worth, and for several weeks to come you should concentrate on the fulfilling task of filling your personal coffers. You couldn't pick a better time to talk to the bank manager, persuade a pal to back you, or discuss a raise with your boss. You can talk about even touchy pecuniary problems with such superb tact and diplomatic delicacy you'll soon have folk agreeing to your every request! Don't let today's successes go to your head though, for you're also inclined to be extravagant.

WEDNESDAY, 27th. Material concerns and artistic acquisitions are happily and harmoniously highlighted by the heavens Wednesday. You have terrific taste, and love to talk to appreciative folk about your treasured possessions. Be sure to turn your thoughts to ways and means of making money too, as you're in fine financial form and can wheel and deal your way to plenty of profit now.

THURSDAY, 28th. Just when you're at your most impatient and impetuous, so sober Saturn calls a halt to all long-term progress and forces you to go back over old ground to ensure there are no overlooked details. Your attitude to world affairs, political developments or religious ideals is placed under an astral cloud from now until mid-October, so you must be ready to think things through on a painstakingly slow, cautious and careful level. For today, watch out for a temperamental outburst that could leave you like the proverbial bull, surrounded by broken china in a shattered shop!

FRIDAY, 29th. You're inclined to be just a wee bit boastful Friday when discussing your cash resources or personal possessions, for you like folk to know what a canny wee Bull you are. The trouble is, an extravagant youngster or spendthrift lover could take you at your word and begin demanding gifts and outings that will stretch your bank balance well beyond the limit. A little extra cash caution today is astrally extremely advisable!

SATURDAY, 30th. Your sense of logic is dissolved and dissipated due to your inability to face up to a few home truths today. You're carrying someone on your back emotionally who's draining you with their hard-luck stories and appeals to your good nature. You're a very gullible Bull right now, and should realise when you're being taken for a ride by unscrupulous folk. Your fiscal foundations are also threatened today by your own extravagant attitude, so if I were you I'd steer well clear of expensive shops.

SUNDAY, 31st. Material concerns and tasteful acquisitions are still uppermost in your mind as your thoughts are filled with voluptuous visions of the lavish, luscious and luxurious lifestyle you would love to become accustomed to! If there's a fiscally shrewd pal or family member around, pick their brains for ideas on improving your economic outlook. They'll be flattered that you took the trouble to ask, and may even have some very useful information to impart.

JUNE

MONDAY, 1st. You're never averse to the idea of talking about money, so if I tell you Monday's New Moon brings an opportunity to reassess your resources and to look at ways of improving your pecuniary performance, you won't be too disappointed. Old solutions to new fiscal problems no longer fit the budgetary bill, and it's time you breathed new life into the management of your money.

TUESDAY, 2nd. Flaming June, as far as you're concerned, is meant for fun and frolics, and even if the weather's not too hot, you're ready to let the summertime swing! This is a marvellous time to join with any youngsters in your world, for their lively spirit and good-humoured gaiety supplies just the merry mood you crave. They say you're as young as you feel, in which case you're a frisky adolescent, whatever your years!

WEDNESDAY, 3rd. A planned journey could run into trouble over a misunderstanding, so double-check your tickets and timetables. Your other half is likely to be much more organised and orderly just now, so why not leave any arrangements to him or her? You can't believe all that you hear today, as news develops diabolical distortions on its route to you. Be sceptical, and wait for the facts before you express an opinion.

THURSDAY, 4th. Detailed discussions, constructive conversations and purposeful journeys should make up your daily activities now Mercury's so ably supported by Saturn. You have the ability to explain your ideas in a clear, concise and convincing way that will win you many influential admirers. Talk to your boss about a raise, apply for a more lucrative post, or contact an up-market adviser and prepare an ambitious plan for your own financial future.

FRIDAY, 5th. You're a sucker for a bargain, or even an expensive item with that touch of luxury you love so much, this Friday. If you need to spruce up your abode with a few choice pieces then this is a fabulous time to give your terrific taste plenty of scope. Don't forget all about cash constraints though! Time spent making your home lovely will bring a warm glow of happiness to your domestic heart today!

SATURDAY, 6th. Let's face it, Taurus, this isn't likely to be one of your best days for intimate dealings with others. In fact you should steer very carefully clear of all sensitive or delicate issues between you and the people in your life. If compromise and co-operation are the oil keeping your amorous wheels rolling smoothly, then you can expect all partnerships to grind to a squealing halt now! You're at your most intransigent and obstinate, and it seems your stubborn mood is catching. Keep things light and inconsequential if you want a quiet life.

SUNDAY, 7th. It may be a peaceful Sunday, but your mind's ticking away, calculating the odds and generally looking for a way to beat all economic rivals. Speed is of the essence in certain fiscal dealings, so prepare your plans now and you'll be ready to strike whilst the iron is hot, whether it's cashing in on investments or approaching someone for a loan. You intuitively know your best monetary move now.

MONDAY, 8th. You've laid your plans, and now's your golden opportunity to begin putting them into action. Your every action today is sure to be constructive, well-organised and positively purposeful. So even if you're not sure of your overall aims, you should set about building a name for yourself and laying respectable foundations in terms of both reputation and financial self-reliance. You're incredibly effective now, so don't waste this chance to set some really long-term ambitions going.

TUESDAY, 9th. Communications really liven up from today onwards, giving you the chance to express your opinions and also to travel for any purpose on a more positive level. At last letters, calls and information will begin to filter through leaving you well advised, amply informed and able to cope intelligently and effectively with just about anything. You're a mental marvel now!

WEDNESDAY, 10th. Your dreams of avarice may feature a pools win or unexpected inheritance but in reality you know financial security can only be gained through careful stewardship and hard work. Those are canny qualities you have in abundance now, so set about increasing your store through putting in for promotion, improving your investments or setting up a sensible savings scheme. Your common sense when it comes to organising cash will stand you in very good stead for the future.

THURSDAY, 11th. All work and no play makes you a deadly dull Bull, so it's a very good thing you're ready to let your hair down a wee bit this Thursday. It may take a certain amount of urging from your more sociable other half, but once you're tricked out in your best bib and tucker and engaged in an animated conversation with someone stimulating, you'll be heartily glad you've made the effort.

FRIDAY, 12th. Anyone glancing at your life Friday would probably think all was sweetness and light, but beneath the surface it's a very different story. Intense emotions are bubbling away with fierce fervour as jealousy, envy and suspicion overflow from the hidden depths of your heart. There are people around you who arouse some very powerful feelings, so try to talk it over instead of suppressing and suffering. It's better out than in!

SATURDAY, 13th. Your taste for all that is grand and gorgeous is a powerful force in your life now, thanks to the golden Sun and velvet Venus, so why resist it? Superbly seductive charm enables you to attract the rich and famous as well as financial fortune and pretty possessions, so use your acquisitive abilities to the full. Music is your food of life, so play on! Socially you're effervescent, exuberant and ebullient, ready and willing to be the star of any show!

SUNDAY, 14th. Fiery, forthright Mars forces his way into your Sun-sign today and immediately endows you with the self-conmfidence and adventurous audacity to push yourself to the forefront of life rather than sitting in the rear. Be active, energetic and assertive in everything you do and you'll shoot to the summit of personal success like a supercharged space rocket! Don't wait for opportunity to knock, for you have the determined and dynamic drive now to take matters into your own very able hands.

MONDAY, 15th. No one could ever accuse you of being cold and uncaring, but it's not so easy actually to express the deep affection you feel for the people in your life. Today's Full Moon brings an excellent chance for you finally to eliminate those emotional blocks and inhibitions. Take a risk and lower your guard, whether it's the vexed topic of sex, money or past hang-ups that needs to be addressed.

TUESDAY, 16th. Yesterday's revelations have certainly loosened your tongue, but the result could begin to sound a wee bit more like a chattering parrot today! It's such a relief to discuss some sensitive subjects, you're inclined to take things to an extreme now and could end up letting slip a few facts that were only given in confidence. It's a marvellous day for an all-encompassing conversation, but make sure you don't overstep the mark.

WEDNESDAY, 17th. Extra excitement is what you crave, and a touch of the unexpected as well would go down very nicely indeed. You will have out-of-the-blue luck this Wednesday, so turn down nothing that could lead you a little astray. The future is bathed in a glorious glow of optimism and hope as you tune into the tremendous potential for universal improvement as starred by the heavens. Give your imagination the freedom to roam over ideas that defy purely rational scrutiny, as your mind works on a more elevated and enlightened level now.

THURSDAY, 18th. Your poor brain won't know which way to turn Thursday as you dream up brainwave after brainwave. You don't quite know where all these original, unique and inventive ideas are coming from, but they've certainly woken you up and put an excitable spring in your step. Wait for a realistic feasibility study before you stake your shirt on some of the more crackpot notions you come up with today. An unexpected opportunity to travel could come your way, but don't set your heart on it until you're actually on your way.

FRIDAY, 19th. Venus glides gleefully into your horoscopic house of sociable comings and goings and interesting ideas, ensuring a pleasant period when you're in delightful demand in your own locale. For a month ahead you're endowed with so much silver-tongued charm you'll have everyone you encounter eating eagerly out of your harmonious hand! For today, however, you can't expect a single message or communication to get through without getting garbled or totally misrepresented. You're just as bad as the folk you're trying to contact as you confuse every issue and grab the wrong end of the stick. Not a good day to tackle important meetings or negotiations.

SATURDAY, 20th. Once the mental mists clear, you're granted a divine day of perceptive clarity when you're able to comprehend the most complicated issues and situations without any trouble at all. Talks aimed at ironing out any worrying wrinkles in your one-to-one affairs may touch on some uncomfortable areas but it's worth it to know you're once again in perfect tune with one another. Don't keep your thoughts and feelings to yourself when there are fond folk just itching to know what's going on in your canny cranium!

SUNDAY, 21st. Midsummer's Day dawns, and you're astrally embarked on a promising period when you project yourself with so much self-confidence and innate authority folk will flock to hear your wonderful words of wisdom. Seize this chance to project yourself on to the sociable stage, and to make plenty of congenial contacts in the community. You don't have to go far, but so long as you venture out into this wide and wonderful world you're sure to meet folk who find you mighty impressive!

MONDAY, 22nd. Prepare to prove to the world in general, and to your pals in particular, just how erudite, eloquent and articulate you are these days. You can open your mouth and spout about any subject under the sun, and you'll find folk hanging on your every word, making this a marvellous time to socialise. Don't get so fond of the sound of your own voice you forget to listen as well, for some friends could have very interesting information to impart.

TUESDAY, 23rd. For a taciturn Taurean you've been mighty talkative lately, and quite honestly you're all talked out! Peace and quiet is your chief craving this Tuesday as you conclude that silence is golden after all. Soothe your jangled nerves with a little mellow music, or stroll in the open air to relish the sights and sounds of nature. You'll soon be back on an even keel.

WEDNESDAY, 24th. Your reputation as a sensible, stable and security-minded Bull is liable to be dented under Wednesday's super-sensitive sky, for you're acting mighty strangely. You're in the grip of some fantastic fantasies and weird delusions, especially where religious beliefs or social ideals are concerned. Crackpot theories you come up with now may well have a germ of truth, but you're just not thinking clearly enough to express them right now. Clam up if you don't want to confuse the issue even more!

THURSDAY, 25th. Your natural sense of ease, equilibrium and equanimity is rapidly and readily restored today by the harmonious heavens, giving you a golden opportunity to get a few routine errands out of the way with the minimum of fuss and effort. Anyone you bump into on a casual basis will prove understanding and entertaining, so take your time as you do your rounds and stop for a chat. You could hear some interesting news.

FRIDAY, 26th. Your very own voluptuous and vivacious Venus is in an astrally auspicious position as she dallies delightedly with both Jupiter and Mars. Your own superb sex appeal is incredibly enhanced, so why not make this an evening for amour? If that's not your cup of tea, set about charming the socks off someone you'd like as a firm friend or associate. Who could resist your affectionate, affable and agreeable advances now? Fiscal good fortune could also come from being a wee bit more adventurous.

SATURDAY, 27th. The chances of a house move or property exchange seem more and more possible now. I would advise you to look very closely at a change of environment as your roots need renewing, and you've the wit and wisdom required to deal effectively with the paperwork and official comings and goings. Chat to your family in the coming weeks and find out exactly where they stand. Where leisure and pleasure are concerned, you couldn't hope for a more enjoyable opening. Take positive action to pursue everything from an enticing amour to a pet pastime and you're sure to make profoundly pleasing personal progress. It's all systems go, Taurus!

SUNDAY, 28th. I know I told you to enjoy life to the full, but that doesn't necessarily mean splurging your entire savings on an outing or digging deep into the housekeeping just to pay for a lavish lunch. Just a little more economy and a little less extravagance this Sunday will make you a much happier Bull when you come to tot up the totals later on! Youngsters with no sense of thrift shouldn't be encouraged in their immoderate ways!

MONDAY, 29th. Aren't you glad I gave you due warning? You're in the mood to appreciate anything that's effective, efficient and well-organised this Monday, and are more than ready to live up to your own most austere ideals. A moderate investment in your career may be justified, though. A superb day for simply dealing with the nuts and bolts of your everyday chores.

TUESDAY, 30th. Fling wide any doors blocking entry to your mind and prepare to give your grey cells an invigorating spring clean! You've finally rid yourself of a few old prejudices and obsolete ideas and now's your chance to think things through from first principles.

Pay close attention to your lifestyle, for if you want to saddle yourself with more healthful and harmonious habits, now's the time to make a start. If you're isolated and alone, you should make the first move to play a part in your local community. You'll find plenty of friendly people just waiting to get to know you!

JULY

WEDNESDAY, 1st. If you're not on your annual holiday yet, at least you should try to arrange for a wee outing to make the most of Wednesday's adventurous, optimistic and enthusiastic sky. An evening spent playing with the kids, pursuing a pet hobby or discussing fantastic future plans with the love of your life will all help to bring a terrific twinkle into your cheerful eye!

THURSDAY, 2nd. Your gentle, peace-loving ruler, affectionate Venus, is caught in a wild celestial whirlwind generated by unorthodox and impetuous Uranus, leaving all Taureans with a sudden fit of temperament to deal with. All at once you're attracted by ideas you'd have condemned only yesterday as wild, way-out and weird, for you're in tune now with the excitement of a much more youthful attitude. Don't go and ditch the old ways or your loyal old friends too ruthlessly or rapidly, for there's really no need to go to extreme. A sudden infatuation may be fun, but don't expect it to endure.

FRIDAY, 3rd. Try as you might, you haven't much hope of keeping your hooves on the ground where they belong this Friday. Instead you're off on a delicious daydream, entertaining the most peculiar notions just as if they made perfect sense. Whilst you're in such a gullible state, don't make any commitments or sign on any dotted lines. Travel plans may be delayed or diverted, so make extra sure of all arrangements, and watch out for light-fingered folk who'll relieve you of your purse or wallet given half a chance.

SATURDAY, 4th. Heave a sigh of relief and prepare to get back to normal. In fact a positively playful mood envelops you this Saturday, so once you've dealt with any pressing business or routine housework, why not give leisure and pleasure a look-in? Whatever tickles your fancy, from a frolic with a ravishing romantic partner to a spot of sewing, painting or gardening, should fill your time very agreeably. You'll be refreshed and restored if you take time for the pleasant things of life.

SUNDAY, 5th. There's a sweet and sugary aura to your world this soporific Sunday, easily smothering any bitter feelings or sour memories that have marred your contacts with others lately. This is the perfect time to make peace with a youngster who's annoyed you, or to proffer the hand of friendship to a standoffish neighbour. You'll easily win them round with your charming smile and words of welcome!

MONDAY, 6th. Mighty Mars makes an explosive astral alliance with unpredictable Uranus today, propelling you willy-nilly into this modern world of technological advance and scientific progress. This is the chance you've been waiting for to buck up your ideas and bring your world completely up to date! At the same time, there are emotional undercurrents to a relationship issue that haven't been adequately explained, so insist now on a heart-to-heart in order to clear the air. Once you've eliminated the points of discord and disagreement, you'll find you feel so much closer.

TUESDAY, 7th. You're still under manic mental fire from Uranus the rebel, who seems intent this summer on breaking down any remaining resistance to the more modern outlook. All at once you begin to see the value of a more up-beat, unconventional attitude, but aren't you in danger of going a wee bit overboard? Traditional ideas shouldn't be disdainfully discarded just for the sake of novelty.

WEDNESDAY, 8th. Where purely practical and professional concerns are involved, Wednesday's stressful stars promise a huge heavenly hindrance. Officials you need to contact can't be found, plans have to be postponed and every effort you make is blocked by red tape. Keep your expectations modest and allow for plenty of problems whilst persevering with your ambitions. Spiritually, intellectually and idealistically speaking, however, you're making much better progress. Seek out folk who can advise you on certain principles, morals or ethics you're questioning – it won't compromise your independence of action simply to consult the experts.

THURSDAY, 9th. A muddled mixture of sunshine and Neptunian mists makes for a confusing Thursday when you're very forgetful indeed. Travel plans or holiday outings could also be affected as you struggle to remember the arrangements and find others are just as hazy about the important details. Your mind may be on higher things, but that doesn't help when you've missed the bus!

FRIDAY, 10th. What you need is a nice peaceful day when nothing too demanding is placed in your way, and that's today's very welcome astral offering. Treat yourself and your other half to an affectionate outing, or perhaps simply a stroll down by the water's edge or through a local park. It's an ideal opportunity to have a pleasant chat about this and that and get blissfully back on to the same easy-going wavelength.

SATURDAY, 11th. Conversations you've had over the past few days have tended to skirt any really controversial issues, for fear of causing offence or even an argument. But you're not so reticent and reserved this Saturday, feeling it's far more important to get your point across clearly rather than worry too much about folks' feelings. For the most part everyone you speak to will be relieved to hear you speaking in a straightforward way and will be only too happy to give you an honest answer.

SUNDAY, 12th. Talks begun yesterday should be continued, for you're mentally as sharp as a razor. You should concentrate on issues affecting your one-to-one affairs, from a vexed monetary question to a passionate power-struggle within your partnership. Vowing to fight to the bitter end won't get you anywhere, but talking about your difference could produce understanding and accord.

MONDAY, 13th. Your own ruling starlet Venus moves gracefully into Leo this Monday, ushering in a domestically divine period when home comforts and happy families take personal precedence. Kinfolk with a taste for the good life could become a bit of a drain on your bank balance, so don't simply hand over extra allowances in the interest of peace. If your home decor's looking dingy in the summer sun, maybe it's time you applied your artistic expertise to produce an abode worthy of your talents?

TUESDAY, 14th. You're under the inescapable influence of today's Full Moon, forcing you to review certain beliefs and convictions you've always held to be true. Look back – are your attitudes and opinions shaped purely by conditioning and upbringing, or have you thought things through for yourself? You'll see certain notions as pure prejudice now, allowing you to drop them from your outlook.

WEDNESDAY, 15th. Your powers of concentration and organisation are simply superb now, as you methodically tackle the paperwork involved in a professional project or get down to the household business affairs. The trouble is, you're so single-minded some folk will think you're cold and uncaring, so try to soften your austere impression and spare the time to crack a joke or share a smile. A hard-working day when you can tackle a great deal.

THURSDAY, 16th. Difficulties in sorting out your personal priorities and domestic duties will make today a strained one for you. Someone in the home or at work seems to be stirring things up a wee bit which will only bring about a battle of wits later. It's up to you to find a workable balance between business affairs and home-based emotional obligations.

FRIDAY, 17th. Your normally placid and peaceable personality could crack from the strain of keeping quiet under Friday's fierce, fretful and feverish sky. You just can't stand anyone interfering with the way you want to do things, and yet certain superiors or bosses are apparently trying to put you in your place. Try not to lash out blindly at folk who rub you up the wrong way, for you're inclined to overreact just now.

SATURDAY, 18th. Thank goodness it's the weekend! You're more than ready for a break, for it's high time you spent an affable evening with your friends. It's important to you today to feel you belong to a close and caring social circle, even if it's just a few pals you bump into at the shops or in your local hostelry. If you're a lonesome soul, join a group or society now and you'll find a warm welcome waiting!

SUNDAY, 19th. Recreation has seldom seemed more important or more enjoyable, whether you're in pursuit of romantic rapture or happily developing a pet pastime or personal project. Just don't immerse yourself in your private interests so much you've no time for anyone else with a claim on your attention. A fantastic Sunday for a gregarious gathering or even a full-scale party!

MONDAY, 20th. Mercury's wandering ways are in astral evidence once again as he hurries off in the opposite direction for a wee detour. It's your home life that's most affected as muddles and misunderstandings accrue amongst your confused kinfolk. Make an effort to note down important dates, appointments and facts, for you just can't rely on mere memory at the moment. Until mid-August you must double-check all domestic arrangements.

TUESDAY, 21st. Look towards the home Tuesday as tranquillity and peace can find their way 'neath your portals. This is a great time for enjoying the glories of your garden, listening to marvellous music and cooking simple but satisfying fare as you need to get that safe and secure feeling that's all-important to your wellbeing. You're a home-loving Bull today!

WEDNESDAY, 22nd. The next few weeks may need extra caution and control, especially in your domestic dealings, but that's not to say it will be a difficult time. You should concentrate on improving and enhancing your security of life. For some of you this may mean looking at founding an enduring dynasty, or maybe considering a more impressive and imposing home. Prepare to play a leading role within the family.

THURSDAY, 23rd. If you're beginning to feel a wee bit cut off from your kinfolk, maybe it's time you had a dinner party or cooked up a simple spread and invited even distant relatives? That may be too much trouble for your lazy and listless mood, but you're sure to enjoy the congenial company of your kith and kin. Even if you simply drop a note round to a cousin or call on your mum for a cuppa and a chat, it'll do you the world of good to keep up your loving links.

FRIDAY, 24th. You could easily earn for yourself a reputation as a real blabbermouth if you're not careful, as Friday's talkative stars loosen your tongue without putting your brain into gear. Rather than spread a rumour or sow the seeds of suspicion why not talk openly to the people involved in an issue that's worrying you? Family affairs will require careful handling, for some very excitable emotions lie just beneath the surface.

SATURDAY, 25th. Mini Mercury comes once again under the icy influence of Saturn, forcing you to focus your mind on purely practical problems. It's not at all easy now for you to get your point of view across to stubborn superiors or obstinate officials, but that's no reason to get discouraged and simply give up. Prepare your arguments with systematic attention and eventually you'll be heard.

SUNDAY, 26th. Financially speaking, things are looking up from today, Taurus! Fiery Mars heads hot-foot for your solar house of cash and currency, bringing the prosperous promise of plenty of opportunity to improve your income through your own independent and energetic efforts. From now until the middle of September you should take all economic affairs into your own very capable and confident hands. Today also brings an excellent opportunity to talk to the family about shared economic arrangements, but don't neglect professional duties simply to chat about the family news.

MONDAY, 27th. I'm sure anyone uttering a thoughtless remark or uncaring comment really doesn't intend to upset you Monday, but somehow you're apt to overreact to just about anything. The trouble is your heart's overruled your head, and purely emotional factors are interfering with your logical view of things. Since you're in such a super-sensitive state try to steer clear of folk you know have all the tact of a ten-ton tank.

TUESDAY, 28th. Sultry, steamy and sexy stars shine on you this tempting Tuesday, and as a result you won't find it all easy to part from your passionate partner this morning! There are people around you now with an intensely emotional outlook and some very deeply felt emotions that you can't fail to respond to. It may lead to an entrancing erotic encounter or a deeply revealing discussion, but either way it will help you develop a new and more intimate understanding.

WEDNESDAY, 29th. You feel much more tense and emotional than usual this wistful Wednesday as you hark back to childhood memories and attempt to relive the past. Much as you may cherish your blissful background and enjoyable upbringing, you can't carry on living in the past. This is your chance to build foundations fit for the future and look for a lifestyle and domestic set-up that suits present-day pressures and patterns. Look to your personal future, Taurus!

THURSDAY, 30th. One-to-one affairs in your world have been undergoing a slow but very thorough transformation for some years now, and it's time the pace of change began to pick up once more. Pluto's positive move today makes for a more definite and.decided approach to making any necessary changes. There may be certain partnerships that are reaching the end of the line, or pressing problems that can no longer be overlooked. Face up to the facts now and insist on an open and honest appraisal. Something's gotta give!

FRIDAY, 31st. If you were feeling a tiny bit gloomy after yesterday's sensitive sky, Friday's optimistic astral array will certainly cheer you up! Opportunity has come knocking, and the riotous rapping is coming from some pretty unexpected corners of your world! Leap feet-first into this modern world, whether it's technological advances, fun-loving fashions or political reform attracting your eager attention. This is no time to play safe or cling to tradition, so be audacious and you're assured an intriguing and exciting adventure!

AUGUST

SATURDAY, 1st. August begins on a high note for you as Mother Moon enjoys the enthusiastic support of genial Jupiter. Make this a weekend for fun and frolics above all, as your merry mood makes you a must for any parties, outings or entertainments on offer. If you're a parent, make a point of spending prime playful time with your offspring – they'll be thrilled to bits and you'll have a lot of laughs yourself.

SUNDAY, 2nd. Are you tired of your kith and kin ignoring your every word and carrying on as if you'd never spoken? Well, now's your chance to stamp a bit of authority on your interaction with certain members of your family, by speaking up and insisting on being given a fair hearing. You'll find they'll sit up and take notice when you really make a point of putting your views across. A splendid day for wide-ranging family talks.

MONDAY, 3rd. You may have all manner of errands to run this Monday, but you know there's plenty of peace and quiet waiting in your abode to help soothe your nerves. The Sun and Moon combine their fond forces to ensure that domestically things go smoothly and happily for you peace-loving Bulls. If you can offer your services to a relative with a bit of a crisis on their hands you'll store up plenty of goodwill as well as having plenty of personal satisfaction.

TUESDAY, 4th. All you crave this Tuesday is to feel as snug as a bug in a rug. You won't want to go out if you can avoid it, preferring above all to enjoy your home surroundings. Maybe you could work from the old homestead rather than brave the outside world? A party or family get-together is on the cards now, or even a wee soirée with colleagues from work.

WEDNESDAY, 5th. The home-loving theme continues with a tense angle between the Sun and Moon, making you even more reluctant to step outside your door to face the stresses and strains of the world. If you can, you'll persuade someone else to step in and take over your duties, but you must go about it with tact and tenderness, for they'll begin to get peevish if they feel put upon. You must be prepared to pull your weight in certain spheres.

THURSDAY, 6th. How long is it since you told your other half how much you care? If there's someone special in your world, smother them with affection and adoration today and they'll respond with warm-hearted happiness. Just don't spend so much cash on showing them a good time that you end up stony-broke! Bulls in search of amour should be prepared to wear their heart on their sleeve on this sensitive day, for your amorous aura could so easily attract a potential partner. A pleasant, peaceful day when pleasure is all-important.

FRIDAY, 7th. You really are an old softy, aren't you? Love is something that you simply need to keep you going, whether it's from a partner, a pet or a child. All you want is to be appreciated, and I think the tender time for all-out affection has come. Don't let a negative superior or discouraging official get you down. They may truly believe you've come to a full stop in your search for success, but that doesn't mean you should adopt their depressing view. Talk it over with a younger relative or energetic adviser and you'll easily overcome official obstacles.

SATURDAY, 8th. The surface of your world may be serene, but how about the hidden emotional depths? Take a peek into the true state of your feelings this Saturday and you'll have a pleasant surprise as you find a complete lack of complications or hang-ups! Whilst you're so much at ease with yourself, talk to anyone with a close emotional tie just to keep up the bonds of affection and let them know you're thinking of them. What a tender Taurean you are!

SUNDAY, 9th. Bulls heading for the sun this weekend are in for a simply super time as you have a chance to find out how other cultures live, and can open your eyes to certain ideals and principles you see as universally important. If you're following your usual routine, make some time to think through your position on certain spiritual, political or religious issues. Maybe your offspring require some guidance, or you're puzzled by a particular problem. You can be sure of coming up with a truly caring and compassionate concern for your fellow man, and a convincingly kindly creed.

MONDAY, 10th. Certain revelations about your outlook on abstract issues affecting your spiritual stance seem to have implications for your personal partnerships. Don't simply gloss over any differences between you and the folk you care most for. If you take the trouble to talk things through you'll easily come to an accommodation allowing for a full range of opinion and viewpoint. It could transform your relationships for the better!

TUESDAY, 11th. Whatever your actual standing in the world, Tuesday's super-sensitive stars make you unduly anxious and apprehensive about the state of your reputation. The slightest aspersion or cutting comment about your professional performance or public position could reduce you to tears, even if it was meant as a joke. Try not to take it all so seriously.

WEDNESDAY, 12th. Potentially this Wednesday is one of the most explosive and uncomfortable days of the year. Every area of your personal and domestic life will be threatened by power struggles and uncontrollable emotional undercurrents which could engulf common sense at any time. Keep a cool head and don't provoke anyone simply to test your strength. Remember, compromise is the true test of wisdom!

THURSDAY, 13th. Take a long hard look at your career – are you heading in a desired direction or simply following family expectations? You must decide once and for all what your aims and ambitions in life are and set out on the path to personal success. It may mean turning your back on past triumphs if you're to move on to future fame and fortune. At last you're able to explain your ideas to puzzled relatives, so set about drumming up family support for your plans. They'll understand so long as you take the trouble to spell it out.

FRIDAY, 14th. What a fun-filled Friday! Friendship takes prime position for your personal priorities as you realise just how much your pals mean. Why not invite the gang round to your place for a wee knees-up? Or maybe you can organise an outing with a group of like-minded enthusiasts? You need to find a social circle where you belong, so if you're still in search of a cordial crowd, join a club or local society and set about introducing yourself. You'll soon be one of the gang!

SATURDAY, 15th. The holiday mood has you in its glorious grip and all you want to do is frisk and frolic in the sun! You certainly shouldn't plan any dirty, demanding or difficult chores, for your heart's just not in it. Look for activities fulfilling your most sophisticated, civilised and sentimental side, from a romantic movie to a classical concert or classy candle-lit dinner. What a cultured wee Bull!

SUNDAY, 16th. Loving lunar rays gleam from your house of dreams and imagination Sunday, immersing you in a sensitive sea of fantastical fantasy and inspired intuition. Memories from the past come flooding back, making this a fine time for reverie, reflection and rumination. Thank goodness it's a day of rest, for all you crave is quiet so you can tune in to your inner world.

MONDAY, 17th. You must have had a very good rest, for Monday finds you fighting fit and methodically masterful. You're incredibly positive, productive and proficient in all practical affairs, from fulfilling an economic obligation to performing a professional miracle. You know the way to make your mark in the world is through hard, systematic work and patient perseverance, and that's the formula that could take you steadily to the very top this Monday!

TUESDAY, 18th. This is a terrific Tuesday for keeping close to your home base as much as possible and surrounding yourself with creature comforts and maybe even a few lavish luxuries! Keep all engagements to an absolute minimum and arrange for plenty of free time simply to put your feet up and drift away into a fantastic world of fancy and delicious daydreams. A relative with a problem will find you so sympathetic and understanding you'll earn their undying gratitude.

WEDNESDAY, 19th. Social surprises set the stellar scene, for there could be unexpected invites or unusual encounters winging their way to you. Don't get all stubborn just because you'll need to make radical changes to your routine to accommodate your changing social circumstances. You've nothing to gain from turning your Bullish back on today's extraordinary astral opportunities, and potentially a great deal to lose!

THURSDAY, 20th. Your very own planet, velvet Venus, is under celestial siege as both Mars and Neptune vie for her attentions. The result for you is a day when you're torn between the positive pleasure of living according to your principles, and the temptation to give in to a fit of fury. Maybe it's undisciplined youngsters winding you up, or a lackadaisical lover with no sense of loyalty. It's up to you to put certain standards of behaviour above your immediate impulse to anger. Go on, set an enlightened example!

FRIDAY, 21st. Every time you try to take control of your home life, it seems someone harks back to the past and you're immediately lost in a sea of recollections and overpowering nostalgia. Don't let purely emotional reasons dictate the way your domestic world is organised, for only by stamping your authority on certain issues will you end up with an abode truly suited to your personality. A very sensitive day for all tender Taureans.

SATURDAY, 22nd. Step into the celestial spotlight and prepare to dazzle any admiring audience within reach! Golden sunshine floods into your horoscope's house of fun and frolics, increasing your creative quotient and boosting your playful potential. For a marvellous month you're in the mood for merrymaking, whether you're keen on the raptures of romance, the pleasures of parenthood or the satisfactions of a spare-time hobby. You're about to enjoy yourself to the full!

SUNDAY, 23rd. Your ruling starlet Venus is entertaining some heavenly heavyweights these days and Sunday brings a close conjunction between Venus and jovial Jupiter whilst also teaming her up with potent Pluto. This all places a powerful planetary focus on your affairs of the heart and also any financial dealings you share with others. Something that began as a bit of fun, or perhaps a light-hearted gamble, could be showing signs of turning serious and if you're wise you won't let that frighten you off. Lady Luck is standing by to make a profound, prosperous and passionate impact on your life, so welcome her with open arms!

MONDAY, 24th. Well, Taurus, it's back to business this Monday as it dawns on you just how much hard work remains if you're to make certain targets or accomplish certain aims. There are obstructive officials who seem determined to make you work like a demon simply to gain a modest advance – maybe they're hoping you'll give up in disgust? Show them you're made of sterner stuff and persevere with your plans.

TUESDAY, 25th. Tuesday is an excellent day for all kinds of communications, but don't expect to get too many purely practical tasks done, for you're all too easily diverted by a pair of sparkling eyes or a seductive smile as you do your rounds! Allow plenty of time in your busy schedule for simply passing the time of day with a few pleasantries and perhaps a little light flirtation and you'll make the most of some very sociable and agreeable stars.

WEDNESDAY, 26th. A major link-up between statesman-like Jupiter and powerful Pluto makes this an important day for your creative concerns and personal partnerships. If you're hoping to start a family this could prove the turning point. Or a romance you've treated as an ephemeral affair could begin to reveal long-term potential. You have very good reason now to feel profoundly optimistic about the future, whether you're facing it as a contented couple or holding out for the hope of approaching togetherness.

THURSDAY, 27th. If your love life has left room for doubt over the past weeks then now you must go through the affairs of your heart with a fine tooth comb. You will also have to take children or teenagers into hand as you will see marked changes in their attitude and approach. All they need is a firm guiding hand and a little well-judged discipline. Watch out for an extravagant impulse if you wander too close to the shops!

FRIDAY, 28th. You may try your utmost to spread a little sweetness and light with everyone you encounter, but some folk just don't want to know. It would be all too easy to take offence and get into a stubborn slanging match, but try to give them the benefit of the doubt. You'll get nowhere fast through simply sticking obstinately to your guns. Concentrate instead on a brand-new hobby or amorous interest holding the promise of much future happiness.

SATURDAY, 29th. Creatively speaking this could be a very constructive day, especially if you have artistic interests. Your taste in all things aesthetic and elegant is second to none now. The only trouble is you're inclined to be a tiny bit languid, listless and lazy, wanting everything handed to you on an effortless plate. Don't squander your superb personal potential just because you can't be bothered!

SUNDAY, 30th. Just because it's supposed to be a day of rest, that doesn't mean you should simply go to sleep. That would be a sad waste of your marvellous mental drive, dexterity and determination, so sit back after lunch and consider your next move in an ambitious pecuniary plan you're hatching. Talk to relatives with an insight into economic affairs, and they'll be happy to point you in a more prosperous and productive direction.

MONDAY, 31st. Venus trots merrily into loving Libra Monday and in so doing ignites your desire to better yourself in some way. Perhaps you feel the environment at work is not good enough for you, or are there health hazards taking their toll on your looks? You've several weeks now to set about introducing some improvements through diplomatic suggestions and gentle persuasion. Prepare to rise high in the popularity stakes at work!

SEPTEMBER

TUESDAY, 1st. September sunlight falls full on your house of leisure and pleasure, celestially supported by the harmonious Moon, making for a very affable and agreeable day. Dull duties and tedious chores fall by the wayside as you fall very willing prey to the temptations of much more entertaining pursuits. Why not treat the love of your life to a night out on the town, or prepare to host a happy gathering in your own home? Fun's the name of your game now!

WEDNESDAY, 2nd. There's a mighty powerful emotional tinge to Wednesday's astral array as the Moon and Pluto combine to promise a sensuous and sizzling slant to your mid-week activities! Grab your partner and take the phone off the hook as this is too good an opportunity to miss! If you're a solo soul then put on your most enticing outfit and head for the social hot-spots. Who could resist such a magnetically tempting Taurean?

THURSDAY, 3rd. The heaven's ever-active messenger, masterminded Mercury, moves restlessly on into Virgo for a spell, endowing you with all the wonderful wit and social sparkle required

to hold your own in the most amusing and entertaining company.
Line up a few outings and excursions designed to give you maximum
exposure and to give you an opportunity to make new friends.
You're about to become the life and soul of the party, Taurus!

FRIDAY, 4th. Quietly, behind the scenes, you have the chance to
get on with some very important tasks this Friday. Anyone looking
over your shoulder would conclude that it's just petty paperwork
and fiddly figures, but you know it makes perfect sense to ensure
your accounts, expenses and investments are in impeccable order.
There's a great deal of quiet satisfaction to be gained from getting
yourself thoroughly organised this Friday.

SATURDAY, 5th. Even the most pedantic, practical, pragmatic
Bull has a soft, sweet and sentimental side, and Saturday's harmonious heavenly parade is agreeable enough to make you feel warm
and amiably affectionate to the whole world! Ideally you want to let
everyone you encounter know just how kind and compassionate
you're feeling, but there are limits even to your maganimous goodwill. So concentrate on smoothing any bumps in the paths of the folk
you know best. You're a real pleasure to have around!

SUNDAY, 6th. Much as you love an established routine and time-
honoured traditions, under Sunday's experimental stars you're
ready to put all that behind you for a wee while. Your pet hobbies
could become really quite off-beat and adventurous as you realise
how many unusual avenues are yet to be explored. Prepare to be a
creative genius! Listen to the bright ideas of youngsters who know a
thing or two about breaking boldly with convention.

MONDAY, 7th. If you have a passionate partner you're in for a
marvellous Monday filled to the bountiful brim with seductive
sensuality and emotional amour! Don't be so preoccupied by your
sizzling sex appeal you neglect to discuss certain long-term plans
with your other half. You're on the same wavelength now and can
easily agree on even difficult decisions.

TUESDAY, 8th. Is your life lacking the marvellous magic of true
romance? Or has a once flourishing love affair begun to fall flat? Put
your most appealing foot forward this Tuesday and you could strike

it lucky in love. Refined rays redolent of romance rain down on you now and enchantingly enhance the affairs of your heart with heaps of harmonious happiness. If you're responsible for the upbringing and education of youngsters, now's the perfect time to try and teach some of the finer points of civilised behaviour and ethical standards.

WEDNESDAY, 9th. Duty calls, Taurus! That's today's starry message, for there's a constructive combination of the Moon and Saturn strictly controlling your overall image and ambitions. You're actually very sensitive about your reputation, but you don't dare show it in case folk think you're not really as tough as you like to pretend. Keep a stiff upper lip and folk will be very impressed with your businesslike attitude!

THURSDAY, 10th. This could be one of the most orignal days of your year, when your mental approach and verbal skills make you a creative and even intellectual genius. Don't turn your tradition-loving back on any ideas or plans that appear eccentric or unusual as it could be the start of something very big for you. Bring your ideas into the fast lane of modern development and experimentation. Fascinating!

FRIDAY, 11th. There are foolish folk who think all Taureans are just unimaginative earth-bound creatures, so now's your chance to show just how wrong they are! In fact you're amongst the most refined, sophisticated and civilised, especially where your understanding of the arts is concerned. When you're not showing your cultural mettle this Friday you should concentrate on the satisfying task of making a respected and well-paid name for yourself in the world. Your every action is ultra-effective now.

SATURDAY, 12th. As Mars makes his positive and purposeful way into your solar house of local and community affairs, so you should be ready to take a leading role amongst friends and neighbours. Maybe there's a campaign that would benefit from your solid support? Friends are very, very important to you now, as they will be able to help you far more than any member of your family. If you are a lonely old Bull without a really true companion then you must try to cultivate a platonic relationship by joining a new social set-up. You could be tempted to cast caution to the winds just to assuage a little streak of loneliness, but there's no point in a futile fling that'll leave you even more alone when it's over.

SUNDAY, 13th. I hope you're not planning a long-distance journey or exhausting excursion for this Sunday, for I'm not sure your health's quite up to it. Maybe it's a simple case of ennui brought about by too many gourmet meals and fine wines, but it pays to take care of your health and avoid pushing yourself whilst you're feeling under the weather. You're much better off spending time with your kids, or talking to a loved one about the emotional underpinning of your relationship. The more you chat, the more you find you have in common!

MONDAY, 14th. There are furtive folk around in your world trying to palm you off with woolly thinking or evasive answers, and quite frankly you're just not going to stand for it! Insist on a straight answer, whether you're talking with someone close to you about the future of your partnership or discussing a child's educational options. By getting down to fundamentals and thrashing out the basic assumptions and agreements you'll soon come to some very sane and sensible decisions.

TUESDAY, 15th. Writing, painting, or perhaps playing music – you excel at anything calling for a creative outlook and certain skills and talents. So even if you're a rank beginner, take your courage in both hands and start out on a course that could take you right to the top of your chosen field. This is an excellent day to chat with children about their own ideas for the future. They'll be thrilled that you've taken an interest and will benefit from a little tactful guidance.

WEDNESDAY, 16th. Look on the bright side today, Taurus, and you could come across some incredibly creative ideas to help you make the most of your impressive personal potential. This is no time cautiously to check out every angle, whether you're about to launch a personal project or looking to expand a pet pastime. Be audacious, adventurous and optimistic as you express your ideas today and you'll win plenty of very positive support.

THURSDAY, 17th. Yesterday's brilliantly auspicious aspect is reinforced this thrilling Thursday as golden sunshine mingles with the encouraging Jupiterian glow. Put private projects and pet pastimes at the top of your personal priorities as you could so easily master almost anything you set your mind to now. Romance-wise you could meet a tall dark stranger, or someone from overseas with an irresistible allure. Whatever tickles your fancy, this is no time to hold back and play it cool!

FRIDAY, 18th. Your eyes have been eagerly fixed on the far horizon for most of this wonderful week, and now it's time you came back down to earth and simply got ahead with a few basic chores and daily duties. Anything from balancing your cheque book to catching up with your laundry or emptying your in-tray at work will give a satisfying sense of keeping your fundamental structures in good order.

SATURDAY, 19th. If your line of work calls for mental mastery and intelligent analysis you'll be in your intellectual element in the coming weeks. Brainy Mercury bustles into Libra today and sets your mind working along purely practical, pragmatic and productive lines. Try to tolerate woolly-minded workmates or confused colleagues, for we can't all be as quick-witted as you. This is a promising period for interviews and appointments if you're looking for employment.

SUNDAY, 20th. An irritable influence from hot-tempered Mars stirs up some very fretful and feverish feelings this snappish Sunday, and almost without meaning to you'll project an off-putting aura. You may relish the odd argument yourself, but anyone trying to cross verbal swords with you will be in for a frustrating time as you come out with peculiar points and irrational ideas. Curb your impatience and try to burn off some of that restless energy in harmless pursuits!

MONDAY, 21st. I know I told you to take a spot of vigorous exercise yesterday, but it seems you've taken things to an exhausting extreme, for you're in a very lazy and languid state this Monday. As the errands and duties listed in your diary pile up, you simply feel more and more like taking things easy. Moderation in all things is my advice.

TUESDAY, 22nd. A very practical period opens up for you now that will help you to get the day-to-day running of your life back into some semblance of order and efficiency. Health problems will also benefit from a more positive and determined attitude. On the occupational front you're eager to take urgent action to improve your position, but more haste in this instance makes less speed, so take your time before committing yourself to a course of action. Uranian vibes are now flowing forwards once again, helping you to formulate a more forward-looking policy.

WEDNESDAY, 23rd. There are demanding family ties on one hand and uncompromising emotional pressures from your partner on the other and you're a very peeved and perplexed piggy in the middle! You'll need to balance with great skill and subtlety on a tense and taut tightrope between opposing factions. You may be heading for a showdown but there's nothing to gain from jockeying surreptitiously for position. Be totally open and honest about the intense emotions being aroused and you'll defuse many difficulties.

THURSDAY, 24th. Fine food, wonderful wines and magnificent gourmet meals tend to be the luxurious love of your life, and you're ready to indulge your tastes to the luscious limit this Thursday! The trouble is it all takes its toll on your waistline and could even begin to affect your health if you're not a shade more self-disciplined. Season every fabulous feast with a generous helping of self-discipline and common sense and you'll benefit in the long run.

FRIDAY, 25th. Amour is superbly starred for the next few weeks and Venusian vibes fondly fill your horoscopic house of personal partnerships. Established relationships are in for an extra divine dose of affection, whilst lonesome Bulls should keep a sharp eye out for Cupid's enticing arrows. Whether in a personal, professional or platonic context, togetherness should take top billing in your approach now.

SATURDAY, 26th. Your overall constitution and health is earmarked for a good check-up according to Saturday's health-conscious New Moon stars. Fitness is very important to your well-being, as you can't do anything unless you've got yourself in good running order. Such a common-sense attitude certainly suits your mood as Mercury's stabilised and steadied by Saturn. Talk to anyone and everyone with an interest in your employment plans and you're sure to impress as well as picking up some very useful snippets of information.

SUNDAY, 27th. I know you've pondered some of your principles very carefully indeed, but the wild and wilful way you're putting them across this Sunday won't win you many supporters. Try to present the bright ideas bubbling through your inventive brain with a little more tact and tolerance. Neptune's confusing detour comes to an end today, so you can look forward to a time when spiritual matters gradually become clearer.

MONDAY, 28th. Nebulous Neptune casts a few tricky traps and subtle snares into the path of meandering Mercury, making you a very sympathetic and sensitive but also an extremely gullible Bull! Mystical, magical and marvellous tales enchant and entrance you, but you must remember to sprinkle a liberal pinch of salt over anything you're told today as you could be open to misunderstanding and even outright deception. Don't be lulled into a false sense of security!

TUESDAY, 29th. Beneath your bluff exterior beats a passionate heart, and this Tuesday it's certainly making its feverish presence felt! You've a tendency now to regard a close personal partner with a very possessive eye, looking jealously at anyone who seems to be encroaching on your affectionate territory. Are you quite sure you're not being a wee bit melodramatic and unreasonable about the whole affair? Give yourself a chance to cool off before you embark on a course of revenge.

WEDNESDAY, 30th. I told you tolerance was your best policy! You'll reap the rewards today of a generous willingness to believe the best of everyone in your world rather than suspecting the worst. It does your harmonious heart good to see folk brighten up when they realise you trust them. A marvellous day to spend time with youngsters who know a thing or two about having fun.

OCTOBER

THURSDAY, 1st. Autumnal coughs and cold are beginning to do the rounds, and if I were you I'd take just a little extra care. Wrap up that sensitive Taurean neck with a nice warm scarf and make sure you stick to a sensible health regime to keep yourself in the pink. Workwise this is a very smooth-running and satisfactory day.

FRIDAY, 2nd. Someone you love dearly has some mighty expensive tastes, and you'd be a fool to bankrupt yourself just to satisfy their whims. It's not in your nature to turn down a luxury-loving impulse but that's what you must do this Friday. A youngster's bright idea may sound superb on the surface, but you must check out the full economic and legal implications before you agree to anything.

SATURDAY, 3rd. Your other half may have come up with a few crackpot ideas in the past but their offering this Saturday is enticingly attractive and immensely alluring. Take a suggestion to get away from it all on a long weekend very seriously indeed, for it'll do you and your relationship the world of good. Whether you've a partner to keep you company or not, maybe you should get away from it all for a few days. You could well meet someone very special whilst on your travels.

SUNDAY, 4th. If you took my advice and tried to get away from it all this weekend, the chances are you'll find professional problems and domestic duties weighing on your mind just as much as ever. Maybe it's your other half reminding you of certain items you've overlooked, or a chance encounter with someone connected with work? The only solution is to attend diligently to certain tiresome tasks before you attempt to enjoy yourself.

MONDAY, 5th. Steady as you go, Taurus! Take the encouraging advice of a loved one or caring colleague this Monday, and don't try to tackle too much all at once. You're tempted to rush headlong into meetings and appointments without preparing your ground, and that'll only lead to stress and strain. You can count on sheer charm to get you out of most sticky situations, but why not adopt a slightly more measured pace and avoid getting into trouble in the first place?

TUESDAY, 6th. As you listen to the news or browse through your morning paper don't hesitate to make a few comments to your other half or a nearby colleague. They'll be fascinated to know more about your personal principles, for it seems you're not quite as predictably conservative and orthodox as they might have thought. It gives you a bit of a thrill to keep folk guessing too, and you may even utter a totally outrageous opinion just to stir up a spirited debate.

WEDNESDAY, 7th. There could be unexpected news from afar winging its startling way to you Wednesday, so be ready to stand firm in the face of a surprising storm. Employment prospects are all at once threatened by new technologies or unexpected developments, but if you stand your ground the effects shouldn't be as drastic as you fear. Until the end of the month you're at least endowed with an excellent ability to communicate clearly and candidly with anyone close to you, from your spouse to a business partner. Communication is the crucial key to all relationships, so make the most of this chance to clear up all misunderstandings.

THURSDAY, 8th. What a kindly old Bull you are! You're under a sympathetic spell as Venus and Neptune join heavenly hands and arouse your most compassionate and caring emotions. For you it's not just a question of looking out for those dearest to your heart, as the universal principles of goodwill and loving thy neighbour means so much to you now. Spread the tolerant teaching and set an affectionate example.

FRIDAY, 9th. This could turn out to be a very tricky Friday indeed, for not only is the Sun set a guileful trap by Neptune but you're being urged on by a rash and reckless combination of impetuous Mars and explosive Uranus. You're as keen as mustard to promote a certain standard and idealistic creed, but every time you make some kind of provocative statement you'll lose your track and forget the point. Keep your head down and avoid the temptation to rush in where angels fear to tread, as the chances are you'll find the ground sinking beneath your feet!

SATURDAY, 10th. Employment prospects have never looked better for all Bulls from this super Saturday. An expansive Jupiterian influence settles into your horoscopic house of health and work for a year's stimulating stay, handing you occupational opportunities on a planetary plate! Whether you're hoping for a junior post to launch you on your career or considering branching out on your own, you've a year's grace to push for improvement. Chronic ailments or petty physical problems should also be taken in hand now your wellbeing tops the astral agenda.

SUNDAY, 11th. Dreams and visions flooding into your bewildered brain this Sunday may be pretty peculiar, but if you think things through you'll see an overall message and meaning. Are there emotional hurts you've hung on to for far too long? Or irrational anxieties that no longer have any real relevance? Rid yourself of them now, and shine the clear light of reason on any muddled and murky corners of your inner self.

MONDAY, 12th. Your fond feelings for anyone close to you reach a torrid climax this week, as your ruler Venus is intimately intertwined with jealous Pluto. This is a time to be extremely careful that you don't use love as a leverage to get your own way, and equally you could fall victim to the emotional blackmail used by someone against you. If there are no amorous complications, you're in for a superbly sexy, sensual and sizzling time!

TUESDAY, 13th. You're in no mood to tackle anything really important this Tuesday, preferring instead to natter on about inconsequential ideas and trivial chit-chat. It's all very pleasant, and fills the time very agreeably, but your incessant talking could begin to get on the nerves of a close partner if you're not careful. Don't be so busy enjoying the sound of your own voice you forget to listen to others!

WEDNESDAY, 14th. You set out bravely to go where no Bull has gone before this Wednesday, and promptly lose your way in a fog of forgetfulness and seductive side-tracks. You may think you're expounding your ideas with crystal clarity, but a quick peek at the puzzled expressions of your audience will instantly put you off your stroke. Every effort you make is apt to be undermined today, so put off important issues for another day. Take any news with a pinch of salt.

THURSDAY, 15th. You couldn't whisper sweet nothings if you tried this Thursday, so don't try to kid the love of your life that you're in a mellow mood when quite obviously you're not! Mentally you're up against a crisis of confidence due to the indifference and carping criticisms of certain superiors or unfeeling officials. Take things one step at a time, make sure of your facts, and stand your ground. You'll eventually get your point across.

FRIDAY, 16th. There's the first heavenly hint of a thaw in the icy impasse prevailing in your professional and public persona. Folk who've seen you purely as a dyed-in-the-wood traditionalist will begin to see your more positive qualities, and value your loyalty instead of condemning your orthodox outlook. Don't look for an overnight turn-around in your fortunes, but steady progress is possible now.

SATURDAY, 17th. Open your eyes to the many marvels of this modern world, Taurus, and heed the excitable advice of a forward-looking friend or progressive partner. Tune in to the news from around the world and you'll soon discover how positive many technological developments and egalitarian ideas can be. On a more personal level, this is a perfect time to chat with a close personal partner to see if your relationship can't be brought more up to date. Maybe antiquated ideas of rigid roles are no longer needed?

SUNDAY, 18th. Are you afraid you may have overstepped the mark with your liberal proposals yesterday? Well, a discreet discussion with someone you care deeply about this Sunday will soon set your mind at rest. So long as you make it quite clear you only want the best for all concerned, you'll soon soothe any tensions. This is a wonderful day to talk over an ethical, moral or spiritual issue with your partner. Two heads are definitely better than one when it comes to working out what's right and what's wrong.

MONDAY, 19th. Prepare to pamper yourself and a passionate partner during the coming month, as voluptuous Venusian vibes stimulate the sensual side of your nature. What a sex-pot! It's a positive period to press your personal interests in an intricate legal or financial affair as your winning ways will ensure you receive a fair hearing and advantageous terms.

TUESDAY, 20th. There are times when you clam up in the interests of a quiet life, but this certainly isn't one of them! In fact you leap eagerly at each and every chance to stretch your mental muscles and give your ideas an airing. Far from resenting your loquacious tendency, folk will be fascinated to find out your true views on a wide range of issues. A brilliant day for getting messages delivered and errands run, and for making useful contacts.

WEDNESDAY, 21st. You're so self-reliant when it comes to material matters you may tend to steer clear of a joint fiscal venture. Wherever your economic interests overlap with anyone else, however, that's where your best personal prospects for profit lie now. Look at legal arrangements, tax efficiency schemes or pension proposals today and you're sure to come out laughing all the way to the bank!

THURSDAY, 22nd. Was it the touchy topic of money, or an unspoken irritation that's set you and your other half at loggerheads? Every word you utter this Thursday will have a powerful emotional impact on a close partnership, and you must recognise that fact. It's no good carrying on as if nothing was happening beneath the surface. Be completely open and honest, but don't be so intent on forcing your own opinions on others you forget to listen and learn!

FRIDAY, 23rd. As the stately Sun sets up in opposition to your own sign for a month's stay, you're given a hefty heavenly hint that your one-to-one affairs should be given some extra attention. Established relationships will benefit blissfully from being placed higher on your personal list of priorities, so why not shower your spouse with wee gifts and tender tokens of your affection? If you're considering embarking on an amour you couldn't pick a more auspicious starting point. You have charm, charisma and innate allure on your side now, so make the most of it!

SATURDAY, 24th. Life's practicalities must be your first priority this Saturday, from catching up with the housework to making sure you get your daily dose of vitamins and adequate exercise. Make a logical list of everything you need to attend to and systematically tick off each item in turn. Some flighty folk would call it dull, but you know it makes perfect sense and thoroughly enjoy the sense of calm control your methodical approach gives.

SUNDAY, 25th. Marriage vows taken now, live-in partnership agreements and professional alliances all round will begin to emerge as very good and positive from today on. Sunday's Scorpionic New Moon marks this out as a wonderful time to begin a new venture with a shared interest. If you still want to go it alone, maybe you should reconsider your solitary stance.

MONDAY, 26th. As the nights draw in, so you're sunk into gloom this Monday, convinced that nobody loves you and even that unreasonable criticism you attract is in some mysterious way deserved. Let's face it, Taurus, you're down in the mouth and nothing I or your other half can say will make you feel better. The only cure for your melancholy mood is a bout of hard work and attending diligently to your duties. Then you'll know you're basically on the right track.

TUESDAY, 27th. Close personal relationships seem to be this autumn's favourite astral theme, and today is no exception. There's a searing spotlight on your affectionate emotions as the loving Moon mingles with potent Pluto. If all's well between you and your love, seize this amorous opportunity to express your deepest desires and most pressing passions. You're certainly a hot-blooded Bull!

Don't let deep-seated differences wreck the harmony when a little open honesty will defuse a stressful situation.

WEDNESDAY, 28th. Ardent and avid affections are superbly stimulated by the sexy stars this wonderful Wednesday, making you a very loving wee Bull indeed! If you've a passionate partner to share your intimate interests you could be in for a very steamy and utterly enjoyable interlude! Fiscal fortunes should also receive your close attention, for by pooling your resources and looking for a more profitable way of sharing your incomes and expenses, you stand to make a pretty penny today.

THURSDAY, 29th. Economic interests will occupy your materialistic mind for quite a few weeks to come, so make the most of this chance finally to get to grips with the intricacies of taxation laws, insurance policies and savings schemes. Talk to folk who are in the know and they'll soon put you right. For this Thursday, you should be ready to take instant and uncompromising action on an item of news coming your way. Lay your plan before anyone else involved and you'll rapidly persuade them of the enormous potential of your ideas. Official backing should also be forthcoming so long as you take the trouble to prepare a properly professional presentation of your plans.

FRIDAY, 30th. Take a bit of a breather, Taurus, for you've put in some sterling service this week and need to wind down a wee bit. Remember one of the keys to anyone hoping to make a success of a particular aim is the delicate art of delegation. Now's your chance to train someone up to take over some of your tasks, or perhaps you should let your other half in on a few secrets so they can lend a hand? You know full well it makes sense!

SATURDAY, 31st. It seems to me someone's flapping a big red rag around under your nose this Saturday, and who can blame you if you let out the odd bellow of pure rage? Calm control and placid peace is maybe your ideal, but they're in very short supply now. Maybe the only way to avoid a confrontation is to take yourself off on an outing, or away from folk who seem determined to goad you. If you're rushing to escape a teasing tormentor though, be extra careful on the roads!

140

NOVEMBER

SUNDAY, 1st. November kicks off with a very positive prospect indeed as Lunar light and Jupiterian jollity exert an utterly enjoyable influence. You're not about to waste such a confident and encouraging combination on mere pleasure, when there are so many practical arrangements to be made for everything from your working week ahead to firework parties and even Christmas plans. You're in your blissful element today, making lists, devising schedules and preparing plans!

MONDAY, 2nd. Are you really being paid according to your true talents at work? Are certain investments giving the return promised? Those are the kinds of questions you should be facing Monday. You can tackle anyone standing between you and pure profit, confident that your easy-going charm will prevent them taking offence or getting up on their high horse. An excllent day for dealing with anyone in a position of power and prominence.

TUESDAY, 3rd. Maybe it's time you let some of your colleagues and companions in on an economically auspicious act? By sharing a snippet of inside information or certain official advice with folk you count as your allies, you'll earn their gratitude and gain even stronger support for yourself. This is a fine time to talk to anyone with a finger in some profitable pecuniary pies. Healthwise you should also consult the experts, who could have some very good news for you.

WEDNESDAY, 4th. The autumn sunshine is blocked and obscured by Saturn's unfeeling influence, leaving you shivering in the chilly shadow that results. For you it's a question of keeping up with your professional obligations and maintaining a respectable public image whilst ensuring that personal partnerships don't suffer. It's a tall order, Taurus, and if you don't forget get a little more co-operation from everyone else involved you're in for a very testing time. Don't drive yourself too hard – it's only human to falter occasionally!

THURSDAY, 5th. Peace and quiet are all you crave, but on Guy Fawkes Day (and Night) that's a bit of a forlorn hope! You could even be tempted to hide away from all the fun, maybe grabbing a sausage roll from around the bonfire and sneaking off indoors to play some soothing music! Well-meaning pals try to shake you out of it, but quite honestly it's kinder simply to let you take a restful back seat in today's explosive excitements!

FRIDAY, 6th. Well, you've had a nice little rest, and now it's time you tackled your tasks head-on in the true spirit of Taurean determination. You're just not content to leave everything to the initiative of your friends and associates, much as you admire their good sense. Take a lead in everything from a community campaign to a charitable cause and you'll find plenty of encouraging support lines up behind you.

SATURDAY, 7th. It seems you've had the good sense to surround yourself with forward-looking, open-minded and up-to-the-minute folk, so take advantage this Saturday of their unorthodox urgings. As they point out the benefits of modern science or argue for an egalitarian cause or experimental ideal, you can see their point and want to express your support. Maybe you can try a few unconventional ideas out in your own life, from planning a more open marriage to befriending someone from a very different background. It'll enrich your life no end!

SUNDAY, 8th. You're oh-so-sensitive and yet superbly sensible at the same time under this sky of rather mixed fortunes. Your dreams and ideals are extremely important to you and your partner now, but at the same time you know an ideal world can't be accomplished simply through fine words and worthy feelings! Point out some of these practical points to anyone preaching a perfect world, but don't let any doubts dim your faith in a better world for all. You're inspired!

MONDAY, 9th. You've been floating in some very ethereal regions lately, and Monday morning brings you down to earth with a bruising bump! Maybe you didn't realise just how much work you've lined up for this week, or has an unkind boss landed you with a task you feel may be beyond your abilities? It's all very worrying, but you won't help anyone if you try to do the impossible whilst

142

suffering in silence. Put your reservations on the record, and simply do what you can. No one can blame you so long as you've done your best.

TUESDAY, 10th. The Full Moon dominating your personal starry picture points to the need for a fresh image and identity much more suitable to your future prospects of success and status! Eliminate any outdated habits or obsolete routines that tie you to the past. Go to it with a more glamorous outfit or a gorgeous hairdo, for it's time to titivate yourself from top to toe. It's time you felt like a brand new Bull!

WEDNESDAY, 11th. You've been getting on so well with everyone from your bank manager or your accountant to the love of your life lately, but Wednesday's wavering wayfarer, wee Mercury, throws a spanner into the works. Every time you try to get a pertinent point across you seem to hit an obstacle and find yourself nattering on about completely irrelevant issues. It's not easy to concentrate whilst you're so distracted, so make allowances for the muddled state of your mind.

THURSDAY, 12th. Nothing pleases a practical Bull more than a chance simply to get down to brass tacks and tackle some regular routine jobs. That's your astral instructions today, which explains the serene smile on your calm countenance! Get your economic affairs into order before the Christmas rush and make sure you're ahead with all occupational obligations. How satisfying!

FRIDAY, 13th. Dire predictions on account of the date have no place here, for I see only positive potential and an auspicious outcome from today's astral event. Venus paces prettily into your solar house of culture, class and civilised sophistication and you have a good few weeks of utter enjoyment ahead! Sparkling social engagements could help any lonesome Bulls meet with amorous enchantment, whilst established relationships will benefit brilliantly from a few extra outings and excursions.

SATURDAY, 14th. Banish those Saturday sighs and weekend worries by spending time with partners, pals and paramours. If a relationship's been going through a sticky patch lately, get to the bottom of the trouble right now and insist on an honest appraisal of what's wrong. Probing into even painful problems will help you to put things back on a solid footing.

SUNDAY, 15th. A little bird could whisper some very welcome news into your eager ear this Sunday, and all at once the world seems a much brighter place! You may have a chance to chat to someone about a vexed economic issue, or shared possessions that are causing contention. With your easy-going charm and enthusiastic eloquence you'll very quickly produce an amicable agreement. Your mind's working along very productive and positive lines now.

MONDAY, 16th. Certain sensitive subjects just can't be openly discussed, but that doesn't mean you should shy away from them altogether. Make a discreet and delicate approach to anyone you sense is troubled, and they'll welcome the chance to unburden themselves. You may have a few revelations to impart yourself, and the result will be a delightful day of total togetherness.

TUESDAY, 17th. As you struggle to make someone close to you understand just how deeply certain feelings run, you'll be dismayed by their flippant tendency to dismiss your worries. I hate to sound a negative note, but maybe you're taking things just a tiny bit too seriously? Take a domestic drama in your stride and you'll find things aren't quite as unsettled as they seem.

WEDNESDAY, 18th. Take a mid-week breather, Taurus, for quite honestly you've earned it! No one's about to complain if you freewheel for a wee while, enjoying the advantages you've so far gained for you and yours without pushing relentlessly for yet more advancement. Taureans with parental responsibilities will also have the joys of having loving and lively youngsters around. And artistic excellence is yours for the asking as well.

THURSDAY, 19th. An active astral alliance between the Sun and Mars gives you the impetus and energy you need to improve all channels of communication in your world. You just won't take 'no' for an answer as you try to get your message across, or ask for an answer from reluctant officials or inactive partners. Take matters into your own courageous, canny and capable hands now and you'll soon get things moving!

FRIDAY, 20th. Now the shops are beginning to fill up with gorgeous glitter and seductive sparkle, so you're strongly tempted to take time off to wander wistfully around the stores, splashing out on little luxuries and exotic items you can't really afford! Take care too if you're out on the town or invited to an elegant affair, for your expansive appetite is apt to get the better of you, and you could all too easily overindulge in the divine and delicious drinks and delicacies on offer!

SATURDAY, 21st. Get down to the nitty-gritty this weekend, especially where your closest relationships are concerned. This is a good time to talk about intimate and very personal concerns between you and someone with whom you share a certain section of your life. Don't hide your feelings now. Mercury's slipped back into your opposite sign of Scorpio for a spell, making it all the easier for you to say precisely what you mean, and to comprehend the moody mutterings of your other half.

SUNDAY, 22nd. You've got that private investigator look in your inquisitive eye this Sunday, which means you're ready and able to do anything requiring a secretive, subtle or spyish approach. The coming month is a good time to deal with joint finances or intimate relationships since you instinctively and intuitively understand just how much goes on beneath the surface.

MONDAY, 23rd. Now don't beat about the bush, Taurus: say precisely what you mean. You won't need much urging to voice your ideas in the most direct and unambiguous way possible, for there's a pointed planetary pairing of Mercury and Mars. Most folk will relish your honest and assertive approach, so make the most of your articulate ability to win the day now. Local trips and meetings should prove very encouraging.

TUESDAY, 24th. Think long and hard about your physical relationships as Tuesday's New Moon heightens your more intimate emotions. Boldly broach any sensitive areas of your private life in order to instigate a new era of understanding and closeness, so don't evade any intricate issues. You can no longer pretend that all's well if it isn't, or your sex life will suffer later.

WEDNESDAY, 25th. Folk who think you're stagnating or even slipping down the slope of success reckon without your uncanny instinct for subtle strategy. It could mean calling on old friends for a spot of advice, or pulling behind-the-scenes strings, but one way or another you know just how to keep your eye on a professional peak or more personal aim. A shrewd investment of cash made now may help your ambitions in the future.

THURSDAY, 26th. You may usually have exquisite taste but you're prone to a few surprises this Thursday as you veer towards the more unusual, eccentric and unorthodox styles. Unimaginative establishment values have all at once lost their appeal, for you want to experiment with anything different and daring. It could mean tuning in to some alternative comedy, looking at modern art with an open mind and accepting attitude, or even suddenly flying off to the sun at a moment's notice. A sudden infatuation may make your toes curl with delight, but don't expect it to endure.

FRIDAY, 27th. As the advertisers keep telling us, shopping days to Christmas are getting fewer all the time, but if I were you I wouldn't plan an extravagant outing today. You may be inspired and incredibly kind in your choice of gifts for friends and family, but are you aware of the precise budget you can allow? Spendthrift Venus is in the seductive clutches of Neptune today, making for a most unrealistic assessment of your own economic resources and the true tastes of your friends. Take the earnest advice of your other half, even if they seem a wee bit severe, for they know what they're talking about.

SATURDAY, 28th. You've become quite accustomed to getting your own way over the past few weeks, but now you must go back over some old ground to make sure you haven't overlooked anything important. Mighty Mars is in retreat from today, and you must rethink many opinions adopted without much thought or deliberation. Don't be too proud to change your mind when need be. Local

146

trips and errands may take longer than expected as you get distracted and side-tracked.

SUNDAY, 29th. Your professional prospects and personal prestige are calling out for your attention this Sunday, so do yourself some good by planning to be much more friendly and sociable with the bosses, bureaucrats and bigwigs. Are your future finances in apple-pie order? If not, spend today reading the small print on insurance policies, investment agreements or conditions for a loan. It's by being well-informed on all monetary matters you'll make the most of your resources.

MONDAY, 30th. November comes to an emotional end as you and someone you hold very dear clash over the direction your ambitions are taking. Maybe they're simply jealous of your successes? Don't just dismiss their anxieties as unworthy of them, for that will only drive them deeper into discouraging depression. Instead encourage anyone who's down to air their apprehensions. You may not have much comfort to offer, but it'll do so much good simply to get the true state of affairs out into the open.

DECEMBER

TUESDAY, 1st. You're certainly off to a super sparkling start this December as mini Mercury makes up his mind to stop mucking about and both the Sun and Jupiter lend their authoritative weight to your personal plans. An enigmatic impasse between you and your spouse or business partner can be resolved now you're on the same wavelength once more. Don't neglect the advice of colleagues, customers or clients who give you the benefit of their generous goodwill and encouraging advice. A splendid day to talk to potential backers.

WEDNESDAY, 2nd. It may be the depth of winter, but there's a sunny smile waiting for anyone wandering into your positive presence this Wednesday, instantly dispelling all thoughts of doom and gloom. Make the most of your winning ways to chat to anyone you want to bring into your ambitious fold, from rich relatives to an influential admirer. You've got what it takes, Taurus, so why hide your light under a bashful bushel?

THURSDAY, 3rd. The heavens are coloured with rapturous romantic hues now, so indulge in any amorous or artistic recreation that makes you feel good. The theatre is especially appealing, as are any creative interests giving your Venusian heritage of the arts and music a chance to shine. You may do a good turn for someone by looking after their kiddie or a pet – after all, one good turn deserves another!

FRIDAY, 4th. As the working week winds to an easy-going end, so you're ready to put even pressing tasks on hold in order to enjoy the less public pleasures of life. No one's going to complain too bitterly, least of all anyone in the fond firing line of your amorous glances and affectionate advances! Or perhaps you're happier wrapped in a cosy cocoon made of your own fantastic fantasies? Give your entrancing imagination free rein.

SATURDAY, 5th. Yet again Mercury's caught up in Pluto's seductive spell, helping you to express some pretty profound ideas to the people you care for. An earnest discussion about the way you relate on an emotional level will help put you straight on some very important points. On a less personal level, this is a brilliant day to set about impressing the powers that be with your superbly prudent and practical approach to worldly affairs. Quietly point out your excellent record and put in a discreet application for promotion. You're such a canny candidate!

SUNDAY, 6th. Under Sunday's super-sexy sky you're passion personified! Your very own Venus is locked in a spirited embrace with ultra-masculine Mars, setting up some very tender tensions and explosive affections. Togetherness is your aim, but you're in danger of dominating your intended amour or companion instead of wooing them. Try to be a little more moderate in your demands of everyone from your kinfolk to your spouse and you'll all get along much better.

MONDAY, 7th. Monday morning blues could make simply getting out of bed a superhuman task. You face the day's challenges with a distinctly jaded air that certainly won't make you a popular choice amongst harassed bosses or stressed superiors. You could really do without all the hassle, but certain duties must be fulfilled if you're to keep the wolf from the door. A discouraging and tiring day.

TUESDAY, 8th. Venusian vibes gleam gracefully from Aquarius from today, auguring an entire month of professional progress and a positive public image. Maybe it's the Christmas spirit, or seasonal goodwill, but even bureaucrats you've brushed with belligerently in the past are about to hold out the hand of friendship. Make maximum use of your innate charm, down-to-earth diplomacy and terrific talents in the coming weeks and you'll make quite an impression.

WEDNESDAY, 9th. Pay particular attention to your entire economic strategy and sense of what's valid and valuable in life, for Wednesday's stars insist unequivocally on the utter elimination of worn-out fiscal policies. Mentally you're certainly on the ball, able to spot an opening well before any rivals have caught on, and energetic enough to act immediately on your ideas. Your usually ponderous pace is sensationally speeded up and the rapid result will be an increase in your own options, opportunities and attainments!

THURSDAY, 10th. I hope you made the most of yesterday's mental mastery, for you're far from reasonable and rational this Thursday. Seasonal messages get you thinking along charitable lines as you dwell on the feelings aroused by certain images and appeals. It does you great credit to be so deeply moved, but it doesn't make for mental agility or logic! Leave important decisions to one side, for your mind's on other things.

FRIDAY, 11th. It seems to me you've been getting into indulgent practice for the fast approaching party season! You know in theory that moderation in all things is the wisest option, but faced with so many delicious delicacies and tasty tipples your self-discipline flies out of the window! You'll certainly feel the effects now if you've been abusing your system, so take extra care of yourself healthwise.

SATURDAY, 12th. Once again, Mercury meanders into Sagittarius and turns your attention to ideas about your shared fiscal future. If there are folk with an equal interest in your financial fortunes, now's the time to set up talks to determine policy. Investigate the details of an insurance policy, find out the legal situation regarding an inheritance or talk to someone about a loan. You've the shrewd mental mastery now to make some sense of it all!

SUNDAY, 13th. Stoke up the fire, stock up on pre-Noel treats and put on your carpet slippers. The home-loving heavens urge you to settle down to some of that domestic bliss you Bulls relish so much more than almost any other Zodiac sign! You're surrounded by warmth and affection at home now and fight shy of any efforts to get you out and about. And why should you stray from your own armchair when it's such a delightful day of rest? Enjoy!

MONDAY, 14th. This is always a hectic time of year, what with cards to send, presents to buy and decorations to hang, but you're in your element. You find the whole exercise really thrilling, especially if it gives you a chance to potter peacefully around your home getting all the domestic arrangements just right. If career commitments keep you from taking an active role, lend as much moral support as you can to folk bearing the brunt of all the organisation and they'll be deeply grateful.

TUESDAY, 15th. Taureans with children under their feet will be getting a touch tense and temperamental this Tuesday, for with all the excitement they're beginning to get out of hand. The only solution is to keep them so busy they've no time to fuss and fret. Steer clear of delicate discussions on tender topics just now, for you're inclined to be irritable and could blurt out a hurtful remark you just didn't mean. A tricky day all round.

WEDNESDAY, 16th. Your nerves aren't quite so frayed and frazzled today, but you're still not back to your usual placid and peaceable self. What you really need is a quiet Wednesday spent far from the hustle and bustle of the world, but some folk seem incapable of leaving you to your own devices. It may not always be easy to keep a civil tongue in your head, but you won't get anywhere by getting all hot and bothered.

THURSDAY, 17th. Yuletide celebrations are known for their gastronomic delights, and you're never one to turn away a festive feast, or even an extra helping of ordinary pud! That pleasurable policy could take its toll on your physical fitness and lovely looks if you don't step in now and take sensible steps to keep yourself in the pink. If you have an office party, friendly meal or business lunch lined up, compensate by cutting down on sundry snacks and in-between bites!

FRIDAY, 18th. Try as you may to get into the festive spirit, the stresses and strains of all the extra activities are beginning to tell on you, leaving you a bit of a nervous wreck by this evening. Let's face it, Taurus, you're trying to do too much, and need to slow down to a more placid pace if you're to make the most of this merry season. Don't be too proud to turn down extra invites, for you must learn when to say 'no'!

SATURDAY, 19th. There, that's better! A wonderful planetary line-up brings bountiful blessings for all, but especially for you as your very own Venus shares Jupiter's lucky light. As your boss looks back on the annum, you'll come in for some heartfelt commendations and maybe a nice bonus or even a raise. Winter ailments vanish into thin air as you realise what a superb celebration lies ahead, and all at once you feel on top of the world! Last-minute shopping trips go like a dream.

SUNDAY, 20th. I don't need to tell you about all the extra little chores and domestic duties keeping you on your toes in this run-up to Christmas but I'm sure you'd rather forget all about it! It's not that you're indifferent to all the excitement, you're just tired out! An energetic other half may have some pretty lively plans lined up for you, and they won't be too pleased if you refuse to pull your weight. Try to explain how weary you feel and maybe they'll let you off some of the more demanding duties.

MONDAY, 21st. What a day! There are four all-important aspects in Monday's sparkling sky, so stand by to make the most of your incredible astral opportunities. Today brings the winter solstice and a shift of attention to your solar house of growth and adventure.

Your mind is filled with improving ideas and a dynamic desire to explore further than you've ever been before. Look forward to a marvellous month of adventure! Don't hesitate to discuss your more daring notions with everyone from your spouse to an interested neighbour. They'll be thrilled with your enterprising spirit and may have some very pointed and perceptive comments to make. Don't worry too much if your professional progress has ground to a temporary halt, as there are plenty of other activities to keep you very happily occupied for now!

TUESDAY, 22nd. Office parties and super celebrations meet you wherever you go this Tuesday, and even if you're intent on getting a few last-minute tasks out of the way you must take time to sup a few festive drinks and maybe munch a mince pie or two! Take the opportunity to let anyone you've worked with throughout the year know how much you've appreciated their support. A divine day for healing old wounds and generally enjoying yourself!

WEDNESDAY, 23rd. Get out a nice neat notebook and logically list everything remaining to be done. Are all presents bought? Will you need more gift wrap? What about extra emergency supplies of Christmas pud and cream? You're an organisational impresario this Wednesday, able methodically to manage the most complex of Noel arrangements without batting an eyelid. Folk around will come to rely on your good sense, and you're only too happy to show them how it should be done!

THURSDAY, 24th. The seasonal spirit is given planetary prominence by Thursday's Capricornian New Moon, shining its loving light on your personal principles and spiritual standards. If you feel Christmas has become much too commercial, now's your chance to speak out for more moral values and to preach the true meaning of Noel. Don't be simply swept along on a materialistic tide when you know in your heart it's time you made up your own independent mind about certain important issues.

FRIDAY, 25th. Your Yuletide sky is packed to the sparkling brim with exultant astral energy and social sensations! You're certainly in for a brilliantly busy time as fond friends and rapturous relatives beat a path to your door just to wish you the caring compliments of the season. With so much excitement you'll be hard pushed to find time to tuck into all the gorgeous grub on offer, so maybe you'll have to call for a bit of hush around lunch time!

SATURDAY, 26th. Settle back on the settee, line up a few scrumptious snacks within easy reach, and ponder your plans for the future. It's easy to cook up some very exalted ambitions and high-flying hopes within the safety of your own imagination, so let your thoughts fly just as high as they like. An idle chat with family members could put you on to an intriguing new ambition.

SUNDAY, 27th. In the aftermath of all the celebration your abode has begun to look as if a bomb has hit it, so set about creating a more pleasant and ordered environment. Don't hesitate to enlist the aid of any willing workers who need to work off some of the Christmas excess, for you're leadership material now and can easily organise a very effective clean-up campaign.

MONDAY, 28th. Some of you will be back at work this Monday, whilst others are just beginning to get back to domestic normality. Either way I don't expect much business to be conducted, for your mood's distinctly mellow and even lazy. You're in your element comparing notes about your Yuletide fun with comrades and colleagues, but much less willing when there's work to be done!

TUESDAY, 29th. All the talk today is about the approaching brand new annum, for everyone you talk to has some very optimistic ideas. Before long you'll pick up on this positive outlook yourself and begin to think along very ambitious lines. Mention some of your professional plans to someone with inside information in the field and they'll offer invaluable advice and heart-warming encouragement.

WEDNESDAY, 30th. As you know only too well, change is anathema to all you bovine Bulls but there may be unavoidable alterations on the way now that you've got to learn to live with. You or your partner may have to come to terms with one of you being thrust into the spotlight, moving another rung up the ladder of success or landing an important job that cuts into your spare time together. With 1993 on the horizon, the only way to move is forward!

THURSDAY, 31st. As you face up to the imminent prospect of a brand-new year, you're wrapped in some very mystical, magical and mysterious heavenly vibes as the Moon wanders dreamily through your solar house of imagination and intuition. Forget all about rational resolutions for the New Year, since it's your intuition that must be brought into play now. Follow a hunch in planning out your future, but don't demand too much of yourself in the way of definite details. What a deliciously dreamy way to drift out of one year and into the next!